A

CHARMED

LIFE

A

CHARMED

LIFE

THE SPIRITUALITY

OF POTTERWORLD

FRANCIS BRIDGER

IMAGE BOOKS | DOUBLEDAY

New York London Toronto Sydney Auckland

AN IMAGE BOOK
PUBLISHED BY DOUBLEDAY
a division of Random House, Inc.
1540 Broadway, New York, New York 10036

IMAGE, DOUBLEDAY, and the portrayal of a deer drinking from a stream
are trademarks of Doubleday, a division of Random House, Inc.

Scripture Quotations are taken from the *New Revised Standard Version*
© 1989, Division of Christian Education of the National Council of
the Churches of Christ in the United States of America.

First published in 2001 by Darton, Longman and Todd

Library of Congress Cataloging-in-Publication Data has been applied
for.

ISBN 0-385-50665-1

PRINTED IN THE UNITED STATES OF AMERICA

First Image Books Edition: October 2002

10 9 8 7 6 5 4 3 2 1

To the memory
of my father,
Harry,
who first taught me
the value of storytelling.

CONTENTS

PREFACE

There are many people who have helped bring this book into being: students and colleagues at Trinity College Bristol who have allowed me to try out some of my thoughts about Potterworld while no doubt questioning the sanity of their principal; Andrew Lucas for sharing with me his stimulating thoughts on children and imagination; friends and colleagues from "down under," who, on a recent lecture tour of Australia, were both affirmative and constructively critical of my views; my wife, Renee, whose interest in Narnia has provided me with inspiration; Katie Worrall at Darton, Longman and Todd for picking up the project at short notice and providing invaluable comments along the way; and, finally, my research assistant, Paul Hansford, who has been a mainstay throughout. I am grateful to them all.

Francis Bridger
Trinity College Bristol
Petertide 2001

THE RIDDLE HOUSE

*An hour later, they headed for Flourish and Blotts.
They were by no means the only ones making their
way to the bookshop. As they approached it, they
saw to their surprise a large crowd jostling outside
the doors, trying to get in.*[1]

I first encountered Harry Potter when I
served as an Anglican vicar on the outskirts
of Nottingham—Robin Hood territory. On
Wednesday afternoons I would visit a local
school to help as a classroom assistant. One
of my tasks was to hear children read. And—
yes, you've guessed it—I suddenly found
myself confronted with a stream of children
reading snippets of the Potter series to me. At
the time, I didn't grasp the significance of
this. I certainly had no idea that Joanne
Rowling's creation was to become the world-

wide success it has, still less that I would end up writing about it. But I guess that's when it all began.

As a theologian interested in contemporary culture, I'd like to think that my continuing interest has been driven by the need to understand what has become not just a literary and cultural trend but a real popular sensation. As the principal of an Anglican theological college, it would be impressive to say that my motivation has been to help future Church of England clergy engage in a meaningful and relevant way with society. As a grandfather, I might want to suggest that I am anxious to know more about a craze that promises to be even bigger and more influential still in a few years' time, when my young grandchildren will be school age and reading books for themselves rather than merely following a story through pictures. As an intelligent and rational person, I could certainly argue that my reasons have had nothing whatsoever to do with the enormous shop window display designed to publicize *Harry Potter and the Goblet of Fire*, the fourth book in the series. But while I suspect that all these factors have played their part, the main reason I bought and began reading *Harry Potter and the Sorcerer's Stone* and the rest of the series was probably nothing better or loftier than a sense of intrigue. I wanted to know, to satisfy my own curiosity, what all the mounting fuss was about. And once I began reading, like the children in that Nottinghamshire school, I found it hard to stop.

ABOARD THE HOGWARTS EXPRESS

In the weeks and months that followed my trip to the bookshop, the hype and controversy surrounding Harry Potter grew and grew. The publication of *Goblet of Fire* had been something of a national event, at times more reminiscent of a carnival than a book launch. Great secrecy had shrouded the contents of the book, such that even the title was under wraps until the week before D-Day. Prepublication sales and orders were so high that *Goblet of Fire* was guaranteed the number one spot on the bestseller lists. Even so, the publisher, Bloomsbury, had still gone to the length of conjuring up a scarlet *Hogwarts Express* steam locomotive for the four-day publicity tour from London's King's Cross Station all the way to Perth, chugging along an approximation of the real Hogwarts Express route. The American film studio Warner Bros. then announced that it would be transferring Harry Potter to the silver screen, starting with a big-budget adaptation of *Harry Potter and the Sorcerer's Stone*. Every detail of the film's production, from cast and crew to sets and merchandise, was subsequently judged newsworthy, trickled or trumpeted to an extraordinarily enthusiastic public, young and old.

Meanwhile, having consumed *Sorcerer's Stone*, I moved on to the second book in the series, *Harry Potter and the Chamber of Secrets*, before embarking on the slightly longer third book, *Harry Potter and the Prisoner of Azkaban*. If the hype and sales techniques surrounding Harry Potter often made me wince, the same can't be said of the books themselves. I found, to my surprise, that I was wholeheartedly enjoying Potterworld. Having written and taught about children's spirituality and faith development for well over a decade, my surprise had nothing to do with the fact that the Potter books are *children's* books. Unlike those bashful adults who were willing to pay extra for paperback copies of the first three books with serious, adult-looking covers, I had no problem being seen clutching a brightly colored children's book, even in the hallowed halls of a university-level theological college. Instead, what surprised me was just *how much* I was enjoying Harry Potter, and how much I was finding to be of real note in the books, both as an academic and as a Christian minister.

Nevertheless, as my enjoyment and appreciation of Potterworld was growing, storm clouds were brewing elsewhere. As a Christian I wasn't by any means alone in enjoying Harry Potter—tens of thousands of sincere Christian mums and dads were, at the same time, finding themselves actively looking forward to reading their children the next installment of Harry's magical adventures as a bedtime story (sometimes whether their children wanted it or not!). Still, opposition from some Christians was mounting, both in the U.K. and America, and also in Australia where Pottermania was just beginning to break out. The Bible, they argued, denounces witchcraft and the occult, and since Harry Potter is all about witchcraft and the occult, Harry Potter must be denounced and the books targeted for banning, burning or (at the very least) labeling with warning stickers. As a result, much to my embarrassment, I found that as a Christian I was increasingly being expected by friends and certain sections of the media to be actively opposed to Harry Potter. I have to say that I could not, in all good conscience, comply with this demand. Not only was I enjoying the books too much but I felt (and continue to feel) that it would be scandalous to write them off simply because of a surface association with witchcraft, when they contain so much of value—both insights and ideas that can serve as a basis for debate and discussion.

Potter fever shows absolutely no signs of dissipating—the final three books are still to be penned by J. K. Rowling, the first film has been released and the anticipation of what happens to Harry as the series continues palpable. What is more, secondary literature on Harry Potter has already begun to surface—both hagiographic or analytical books like this one, and what we must hope will be the first of many companion works by Rowling herself (*Quidditch Through the Ages*, written under the penname Kennilworthy Whisp, and *Fantastic Beasts & Where to Find Them*, written under the name Newt Scamander, both created and sold in aid of the charity Comic Relief). Harry Potter has all the makings of a classic and there's every reason to believe that Rowling's creation will be as read and loved in fifty years' time as C. S. Lewis's Narnia books (currently enjoying their golden jubilee) are now.

CRACKING THE CODE

This book is not written in praise of Harry Potter, though it does indeed contain a great deal of praise. Nor is it written in reproach, though it contains a little bit of that as well. I write as a theologian, a Christian, a pastor and a grandparent, and find myself engaging with Potterworld on all four levels. The books, not to mention the extraordinary and at times obsessive following they've attracted, offer us a snapshot of contemporary society, good and bad. For me, this is their most valuable attribute, and my principal reason for writing. Like all good stories, the Potter books not only keep us thoroughly entertained, they also tell us a considerable amount about ourselves—our characters, our relationships, our priorities, our communities and even our spirituality.

Of course, explaining all this isn't straightforward. Unlike Lewis's world of Narnia, Potterworld isn't allegorical. There's no simple equivalence between Lord Voldemort and the devil, for instance, as there is between Aslan and Christ in *The Lion, the Witch and the Wardrobe*. The symbols, imagery and plots used in the Potter books, and the issues dealt with, are more complex than those in Lewis's groundbreaking work. They present us, to some extent, with what Churchill (speaking about Russian foreign policy at the outbreak of World War II) called "a riddle wrapped in a mystery inside an enigma."

The conclusions I've reached, therefore, are in many ways subjective ones. They are what have struck me personally during the course of my reading. I certainly don't imagine, for example, that every Potter reader will have seen in the wizard jail Azkaban a reflection of the Christian idea of hell, or that Joanne Rowling had hell in mind when she created Azkaban. (As we'll see, she actually had something else in mind.) Nevertheless, Azkaban *does* provide us with a window into hell—a way of exploring the bundle of themes that have traditionally been grouped around the doctrine, as well as the various secular equivalents that have come to take the place of hell in what is now increasingly a post-Christian society. In Azkaban, as in so much else in Potterworld, we can see not just the vestiges of a largely disappearing Christian worldview but also some of the new ways people have found for expressing and exploring the kind of key spiritual issues (justice, judgment and the debilitating effects of evil) that, a century ago, were clustered around established views of heaven, hell and eternal damnation.

A last word: In interviews, articles and reviews, the majority of writers and journalists—as well as Joanne Rowling herself—have been very careful to avoid giving away too much of the plot of the books so as not to spoil the enjoyment of first-time readers. Even when it became clear that a favorable character would die in the fourth book, for example, considerable care was taken *not* to say which one. In a book like this, however, which aims to discuss the Potter series in some detail, that kind of circumlocution is simply impossible. I apologize in advance if this hinders your subsequent enjoyment of the novels, like knowing the identity of the murderer before embarking on a "whodunit" story. All I can say by way of defense is that, since the books hold up extremely well to a second reading—as I myself and literally millions of children will testify—I won't have spoiled *all* your enjoyment by giving things away.

chapter one

THE DARK MARK

DEMONIC CREATION
OR DAREDEVIL HERO?

*At this very moment, people meeting . . . all over
the country were holding up their glasses and saying in bushed voices: "To Harry Potter—the boy
who lived!"*[1]

The Potter phenomenon has not only been
unbelievably successful, it has aroused unbelievably strong reactions. Take, for example,
the case of the principal of a small Kent
school who in early 2000 suddenly found herself the focus of both local and national media
attention when her concern over the effect of
stories about witchcraft and wizardly on
young, impressionable minds prompted her
to ban the Harry Potter books from lessons
and activities on school property. A committed Christian, she didn't want to be seen as
giving the nod to anything that treated witch-

craft either lightly or positively. "We are a Church of England–aided primary school," she told reporters, "which means the Church ethos is very important to what we do. The Bible is consistent in its teachings that wizards, devils and demons exist and are real and dangerous, and God's people are told to have nothing to do with them."[2] While not going so far as to forbid pupils to have their own copies of the books in school, she nevertheless tried to draw a firm line, making it very clear to all those in her care that both she and the school's governors frowned heavily on Joanne Rowling's literary output, together with anything and everything else that portrayed witches and wizards as "fantasy, imaginary, fun and harmless."

Public reaction to her ban varied enormously, and spread well beyond the confines of the school gates into the local community and (for a time, at least) most of the country. Some parents, concerned citizens and religious leaders entirely applauded her decision, sharing her fears that Harry Potter was the thin end of a wedge that could result in full-blown involvement in the occult and witch covens for some pupils, and a blindness to the potential risks for others who would see the occult as essentially a harmless, danger-free zone. Most people, however, seemed to feel that the ban was unwarranted, to say the least. Some were amused by what they saw as just a silly overreaction. Others expressed less generous, and perhaps unfair sentiments: outrage at such blatant efforts at censorship, or scorn and antipathy at what they considered the teacher's "fundamentalist" brand of Christian views.

The newspapers, by and large, portrayed her as a fairly mild-mannered crackpot. They didn't question the sincerity of her motives but they *did* seriously doubt the soundness of her judgment.[2] Some even took her assurances that she had full support from the school's parents as a direct challenge to find dissenting mums and dads. At any rate, few other principals—including heads of Church schools—endorsed the ban, and no school implemented similar measures. In fact, in a nationwide survey of primary and secondary principals done later in 2000 in conjunction with The Stationery Office, over ten percent admitted that they saw Albus Dumbledore, head of Rowling's Hogwarts School of Witchcraft and Wizardry, as something of a role model!

The Kent principal, however, was far from the only one with strong views. In other English-speaking countries, for instance, reactions have been just as extreme—positive and negative. Among supporters, enthusiasm has been high. On the eve of the U.S. publication of *Azkaban* and *Goblet of Fire*, many bookstores—not permitted to sell copies before the official publication dates—threw Potter parties, complete with cakes, costumes and a countdown to midnight, so eager young readers wouldn't have to wait the eight or nine hours until morning. Instead, they could get their hands on a copy just minutes after it went on sale. Similarly, when Rowling toured the U.S. in September 1999 to promote *Azkaban*, young Potterphiles pestered their parents and stood in line for hours outside stores in full costume—pointy hat, round glasses, a robe and a flash of lightning on the forehead—just for the chance to get a signed copy.

But negative reactions were just as frenetic. Shortly after the U.S. release of *Azkaban*, anxious parents in South Carolina petitioned the state Board of Education to withdraw Harry Potter from elementary and junior high school libraries and reading lists. One mother, invited to address the Board in person about her concerns, told reporters she felt the books contained "a serious tone of death, hate, lack of respect and sheer evil."[3] The Board's minutes reduce her impassioned plea to a matter-of-fact line swamped by other business—a "concerned parent" spoke "regarding the use of certain books in schools"[4]—and the

Board itself opted to do no more than review the suitability of the books for the schools in its jurisdiction. Nevertheless, the mother's words helped to galvanize opposition to Harry Potter across the nation.

Parents and school administrators in neighboring Georgia—as well as in non–Bible Belt states such as Michigan, Minnesota, New York and California—tried to have the Harry Potter books removed from the shelves of their local school or public libraries, or axed from the curricula. In fact, the American Library Association reports that there were more attempts to ban Harry Potter from libraries during 1999 than any other book, even though *Chamber of Secrets* and *Azkaban* were only published in the U.S. in June and September of that year, and *Goblet of Fire* didn't come out until July 2000. Reasons given were to do with the supposed "focus on wizardry and magic" in the books. Canada similarly found itself experiencing Potterphobia: After pressure, a school board near Toronto briefly ruled that primary school pupils in its district would have to bring permission slips before Harry Potter could be read aloud in class. And in Australia, anxious parents and certain Christians petitioned to have stickers put on all copies of the books, warning all buyers and readers about the potential unsuitability of the contents. As late as April 2001, a fundamentalist group in rural Pennsylvania was reported to have burned the series in public along with videos of *Pinocchio* and *Hercules*.

For her part, Joanne Rowling hit back at the widely reported allegations that her books corrupted children or encouraged occult involvement. "I have yet to meet a single child who's told me that they want to be a Satanist or are particularly interested in the occult because of the book[s]," she explained. Given her reclusive tendencies (she gave almost no interviews for the British release of *Azkaban*, and agreed to promote *Goblet of Fire* only because she knew that there was no way to avoid the media circus'), we might be tempted to take this comment with a large pinch of salt. However, the sheer volume of fan mail she has received from enthusiastic readers in over forty countries should give us pause. The amount of positive feedback she has experienced has, at times, been overwhelming: After the success of *Azkaban* she had to move out of her besieged terraced house in Edinburgh into a part of the city that could provide her and her daughter with more privacy and protection.

Mostly, children want to express their enjoyment and beg her to keep on writing. But when U.S. publisher Scholastic launched a competition asking children to say "How the Harry Potter Books Changed My Life," they received essays explaining how Harry, Ron, Hermione or one of the books' other characters had helped them to cope with illness, abuse, bullying or rock-bottom self-esteem. No one has yet suggested that they want to become a real-life witch or wizard (though one or two, especially among the books' older readers, may well fancy becoming the driver of Hogwarts' magical steam locomotive, the Hogwarts Express).

Nevertheless, staunch opposition to Harry Potter has continued almost as persistently and aggressively as the books themselves have continued to sell. Worried parents have tried to protect their children from what they perceive as a real threat, while many Christians and Church leaders have struck out against books they consider to stand (in the words of one e-mail correspondent to *Time* magazine's website) "in direct conflict with Christianity."

The release in July 2000 of the eagerly awaited and overly hyped *Goblet of Fire* added more fuel to this well-stoked furnace. If parents in South Carolina had been worried by the "serious tone of death, hate, lack of respect and sheer evil" pervading the first three books, *Goblet of Fire* must have confirmed their worst fears. The opening chapter, Rowling's darkest piece of writing to date, undoubtedly *does* contain a "serious tone of death, hate, lack of respect and sheer evil." In fact it contains two *actual* deaths—one reported and one described (though in true Hitchcock style, the menace is conveyed entirely by suggestion, rather than by any kind of graphic or grisly detail). It also contains the presence, in the flesh, of the villain of Potterworld, the virtual apotheosis of evil, Lord Voldemort. All in all, it heralds a shift in the mood of the series—a genuine darkening of the atmosphere. It ends, 630 pages after its grim beginning, with a kind of *Walpurgisnacht*: the renaissance of Voldemort's feared henchmen, the Death Eaters, together with a dramatic showdown between Harry and Voldemort himself, the senseless death of Cedric Diggory and an effective declaration of war between the forces of good and evil. And as if that weren't enough, the title of the final chapter, "The Beginning," hints at even darker things to come in the saga's three remaining books.

THE BOGGART IN THE WARDROBE

Opposition to Harry Potter in both the U.S. and the U.K. has tended to focus, without any real distinction, on two specific issues: the darkness of the novels, and their apparent endorsement of magic and witchcraft. For many parents, it is not just that the books are too scary for young children, they are actually working to undermine "good Christian values."

In somewhere as secularized as Britain—where although 65 percent of the population sees itself as Christian, only about 8 percent can actually be found in church on any given Sunday morning—it is easy to imagine that an insistence on uniformly "Christian values" being implemented In society is the preserve of just a tiny, if vocal, "funda mentalist" minority. However, in terms of churchgoing and overt adherence to religious values, the U.S. is an apparently more "Christian" country than Britain—perhaps as much as 60 percent of the population not only calls itself Christian but regularly attends church. "Christian values," in other words, aren't just the moralistic crusade of the few but the basic moral framework of the many. So it is easy to understand how some anxious parents could interpret Potter wizardry as undermining the values of American society as a whole.

Unfortunately, objections to witchcraft on the grounds of "good Christian values" have something of a sordid history. Between about 1380 and 1680, as many as 40,000 people, mostly women, were burned for witchcraft in Europe, including up to 1,000 in England and 1,600 in Scotland. Most were executed after the medieval equivalent of "due process" of law. As historian Barbara Tuchman wrote, "Medieval justice was scrupulous about holding proper trials and careful not to sentence without proof of guilt but it achieved proof by confession rather than evidence, and confession was routinely obtained by torture."[6] England's "enlightened" alternative to the use of torture was no better: Suspected witches were bound hand and foot and dropped into a river; those who drowned were pronounced posthumously innocent, while those who survived such certain death (aided, of course, by the devil) were promptly executed! There were no purges in England after 1680 but witchcraft remained a capital offense until 1737 and a popular obsession for some decades afterward.

The most famous witch-hunt of all, of course, took place in Salem, Massachusetts, in 1692. When a group of girls began to scream, convulse and bark like dogs, Salem's townsfolk suspected they had been bewitched. When this and other strange forms of behavior spread, people were gripped with fear that Satan himself had come to town. A full-scale witch-hunt was initiated and a special court set up to investigate. Since the threat faced was supernatural, the court accepted as all-but-conclusive proof of guilt the presence of warts or protrusions on a suspect's body (witch's teats to suckle a familiar), as well as spectral evidence that suspects had tortured people in their dreams. Those suspects indicted with such undeniable evidence who then "confessed" their heinous crimes were spared death but those who stubbornly continued to insist on their innocence were dealt with harshly. Within a year, nineteen people had been executed for witchcraft. Significantly, *no one* who stood trial was found not guilty. However, when the hysteria died down, the townsfolk began to question the safety of these convictions. Most of the remaining suspects were subsequently acquitted and the Massachusetts governor pardoned all those who weren't. Today, every one of the convictions is considered unsafe.

Any serious attempt to object to the Potter books on the grounds of their supposedly endorsing witchcraft will, of course, inevitably have to live in the shadow of this rather sordid history of witchhunting and learn from its mistakes. It is not for nothing that the term "witch-hunt" now has negative rather than positive connotations. The desire to protect society from demonic power, linked to a very real fear of the devil himself, hasn't always brought out the best in those most concerned to promote "good Christian values." Potterphobes take note: Fear has all too often outweighed fact and a careful scrutiny of the evidence. No one, of course, has yet suggested burning Joanne Rowling at the stake, or subjecting her to a float-test, but most of the reaction against her books—fueled by a praiseworthy desire to protect children from potentially harmful influences, and by a genuine fear of the demonic—has failed to examine closely enough both the evidence from the books themselves and the consistency and logic of the arguments used against them.

"The only thing we have to fear is fear itself," Franklin D. Roosevelt reassured a public gripped by the Great Depression, in his first inaugural speech in 1933. They were wise words. In fact Rowling herself has made use of them. In *Azkaban*, Defence Against the Dark Arts teacher Remus Lupin introduces his third-year class to a Boggart—a mischievous pest of a shape-shifter that can, in Hermione's predictably accurate description, "take the shape of whatever it thinks will frighten us most."[7] As Lupin explains, Boggarts inhabit dark, enclosed spaces—the area beneath the bed, for example, or, as his class discovers for itself, the inside of the staffroom closet. Boggarts have no real shape of their own but assume instead the form of what most terrifies the people they come into contact with. In Potterworld, they represent in its most basic form our very fear itself.

For Neville Longbottom, the Boggart in the closet automatically takes the form of Professor Snape. Nothing and no one, for poor Neville, is quite as terrifying and intimidating as the Hogwarts' Potions master. For Ron, it is a hairy, six-foot, human-eating spider. His natural fear of spiders, shared by many of the class, was considerably magnified by his narrow brush with death at the hands—or rather, pincers—of Aragog and his fellow outsized arachnids in *Chamber of Secrets*. For Lupin and Harry, the Boggart's transformation is slightly different: Rather than directly taking the form of what they fear, the Boggart takes a form that *represents* their fear. For Lupin, it becomes a rather mystifying "silvery white orb hanging in the air." As the book later makes clear, this is a miniature moon: Every month, under the full moon, Lupin turns into a werewolf and runs amok. What frightens him, however, isn't the moon itself but his own murderous potential—unless he is restrained (at first physically by being imprisoned in the Shrieking Shack, then later through the presence of his three Animagus friends, and in more recent times chemically by means of a special potion), he will prey unwittingly on man and beast. For Harry, the Boggart turns itself into a soul-sucking Dementor.

Real discussion of the Dementors will have to wait until Chapter Four. For now, what matters is Harry's fear of them. Assuming that what Harry fears most is actually Voldemort, Lupin intervenes in class before it gets to be his turn to confront the Boggart. "I didn't think it a good idea for Lord Voldemort to materialize in the staff room," Lupin explains. "I imagined that people would panic."[8] When Harry admits that he *had* initially thought of Voldemort but had then realized that he feared the Dementors even more, Lupin is impressed. "That suggests that what you fear most of all is—fear," he remarks.[9] For Harry, the Dementors represent a greater threat even than Lord Voldemort because he doesn't know how to combat them. Their appearance, whether in the Hogwarts Express train or on the Quidditch pitch, disarms Harry completely, overcome by the buried memory of his parents' cruel death at Voldemort's hands. Their soul-sucking abilities rob him of his strength in a way that even Voldemort doesn't. As Lupin explains, "The Dementors affect you worse than the others because there are horrors in your past that the others don't have."[10] The Dementors prey on this horror, amplifying it and feeding on it, and Harry's inability to confront them—to confront his own fear and past horror—makes them the thing that frightens him the most. Almost literally, the only thing he has to fear is fear itself.

In a way, the Potter books act rather like a Boggart: The threat they represent is defined by the fears people bring to them. Those most frightened by the potential danger of witchcraft and the occult see in Harry Potter the thin end of a wedge that will lead inevitably into coven membership and demonic possession. Those most frightened by the very real possibility that their own or other people's children will be in some way abused or corrupted by society see in the books a slippery slope into a contaminated culture. Those who themselves fear death, evil and the psychological equivalent of gnarling monsters under the bed see in the increasingly lurid ambience of Potterworld "a serious tone of death, hate, lack of respect and sheer evil." What they are seeing isn't Harry Potter, but a Boggart: an inherently shapeless representation of their own fears.

By saying this, I am not trying to belittle those fears, or the concerns and motivations of those who, generally with the best of intentions, have fired a broadside at Harry Potter. One of the things that the incident of the Boggart in the closet makes clear—abundantly clear—is that fears are powerful influences and that left unchecked they can be soul destroying. Fears need to be confronted. In fact as we shall see in the next chapter, one of the reasons why I'm so positive about Harry Potter is precisely because it gives children (and adults) the chance to face their fears and begin to tackle them within a safe environment. It is good for the issues of child safety, social corruption, death and even the demonic to be given a higher priority on the public agenda, since they are frequently ignored. (In his satirical book *The Screwtape Letters*, C. S. Lewis warned of the twin dangers on the one hand of entirely dismissing the seriousness of the demonic, and on the other hand of taking it too seriously.) However, there is a great difference between using the Potter books as a convenient starter for a discussion of the occult or of amorality in children's literature, for example, and attacking it for actually *endorsing* the occult or *being* amoral (or even *im*moral). The first is justified, even beneficial. The second is in reality nothing more than an attack on a Boggart, driven by fear divorced from fact.

"IT AIN'T NECESSARILY SO . . ."

Take the negative reaction that Harry Potter should be opposed, at least by Christians, because it is fundamentally a tale about witchcraft and the occult. This was the response of the Kent principal, among others. "The Bible is consistent in its teachings that wizards, devils and demons exist and are real and dangerous," she told reporters, explaining her ban on the Potter books. "God's people are told to have nothing to do with them." Half a world away, ignorant of the shenanigans in Kent, a correspondent to *Time* magazine's website agreed. "From reviews I have read, Harry is a warlock, or male witch. In this [he] is in direct conflict with Christianity."

If these comments were true and relevant to Harry Potter, there would indeed be some cause for concern, at least for Christians. They are, however, wide of the mark. The wizardry and witchcraft of Potterworld is a fictional device, quite different in its tone and content from the wizardry and witchcraft that stand in conflict with Christianity. For example, Rowling is careful *not* to describe Harry as a "warlock." Although—or rather, I think, *because*—this is the technically correct term, she uses it very rarely and never in reference to Harry, preferring instead the more fanciful and fictive term "wizard."

Rowling's choice of words usually seems to be deliberate, especially when it comes to names. Some sound funny or particularly appropriate: Slytherin and Hufflepuff, for example, are onomatopoeic names for the school houses represented in Hogwarts' heraldry as a snake and a badger, and Professor Sprout is well named for an Herbology teacher. Others, however, appear to have a rather deeper meaning: The name of Harry's school nemesis, Draco Malfoy, for instance, breaks down into the Latin for "snake" and "bad faith"; his Animagus guardian Sirius Black, who has the ability to turn himself into a black dog, is named after Sirius, the bright "dog star" in the

Canis Major constellation; werewolf teacher Remus Lupin is named after the Latin for "wolf" and the name of one of Rome's two mythological founders, suckled by a she-wolf; Potions master Severus Snape's name derives from the Latin for "severe" and an English word meaning "chide" or "rebuke"; house-elf Dobby's name is a late seventeenth-century English term for a "dunce" and a late eighteenth-century term for a household spirit. (It is, of course, possible to take this kind of analysis too far: There is as yet no evidence to link Hogwarts' headmaster Albus Dumbledore with albino bumblebees, even though *albus* is Latin for "white" and "dumbledore" is a sixteenth-century English term for a bumblebee; nor is there any suggestion that the school's motto—*Draco dormiens nunquam titillandus*—should be translated "Never rouse a dormant snake" rather than the less ominous but much funnier "Never tickle a sleeping dragon"!)

By choosing "wizard" Rowling creates a more fanciful, frivolous tone than she would have done if she had opted for "warlock." "Wizard," a medieval word derived from "wise," is linked to centuries of folklore and storytelling rather than modern witchcraft. It is also a word in common use—"financial wizard" or "technical wizard," for example. Having decided, in other words, to use magic in her stories, she would appear to have opted for the storyteller's brand of magic rather than the more serious occult brand of magic.

But is this a meaningful distinction? Are there really "occult" and "nonoccult" types of magic—harmful ones of fact and harmless ones of fiction? Regardless of the words Rowling uses to describe what her characters do, and her own desire to tell a story rather than promote serious witchcraft, doesn't the very presence of magic and witchcraft in Potterworld stand "in direct conflict with Christianity"? I believe the answer to this question has to be *no*. Though there is—in the Bible, for instance—a clear distinction between damnable "magic" on the one hand and divine "miracle-working" on the other, they can, on the surface, look remarkably alike.

The patriarch Joseph, for example, had a God-given talent for interpreting dreams—a skill that would have seemed "magical" to his Egyptian overlords. From their perspective, dreams were one of the principal means by which Egypt's gods communicated their will and desire to their human subjects. Similarly, Moses' God-given ability to turn Aaron's staff into a snake, and to predict the plagues, would have been seen by Egypt's wizards ("wise men") as incidents of pagan magic, worked by skill through the power of Egypt's own "gods." Even the miracles of Jesus were seen by many as having been wrought by demonic power: "He has Beelzebul," they said, "and by the ruler of the demons he casts out demons."[11] They didn't doubt the *reality* of his exorcisms but they did suspect him of witchcraft and wizardry. In the words of the second-century Christian writer Justin Martyr, "Those who saw these events taking place alleged that it was a magical illusion, and indeed they dared to call him a sorcerer and a deceiver of the people."[12] Jewish rabbis later recorded the charge against Jesus as it came down to them: "He has practiced sorcery and enticed Israel to apostasy."[13]

Of course, readers of Genesis, Exodus and the Gospels know, thanks to the benefit of hindsight, what was far from obvious to contemporary observers: that Joseph, Moses and Jesus were performing "miracles" by the power of God rather than pagan "magic." But as New Testament scholar Tom Wright puts it, "Jesus does seem to have used techniques, in performing cures, which his contemporaries might well have regarded as magical."[14]

In fact in the most famous instance of "wizardry" in the Bible, the wizards themselves receive honorable mention. As anyone who has ever been to a nativity play knows, men came from the east to see Jesus after his birth. The New Testament doesn't tell us their names,

nor that they were kings, nor even how many of them there were—
"We Three Kings of Orient Are" is the fanciful invention of a much
later age. But Matthew's Gospel (the only one to record their arrival)
does give us an extraordinary detail: They were "wise men"—"wise-
ards" or "wizards."[15] They are sometimes called "magi" (which gives
us the English "magic" and "magician"), the Latin version of
Matthew's ancient Greek word. They weren't Jews or Christians:
They came from the Parthian Empire and dabbled in the branch of
wizardry we would now call "astrology."

So where does this leave the magic of Harry Potter? For a start,
"devils and demons" are nowhere to be found in Potterworld. Magic
merely seems to be a force or an instrument that characters use in
rather the same way we use electricity. Unlike the magic condemned
in the Bible, Potterworld magic doesn't symbolize or flow from a supernatural or demonic realm in opposition to God: It is simply *there*.
It is part of the natural (and sometimes even mundane) order of wizard reality. In short, it remains a literary device to thrill the reader,
and to allow the author to create an alternative world unbound by the
laws of physics.

In this respect, it is comparable to the equally unscientific and
quasi-magical powers of literary creations such as Superman. For all
the pseudoscience put forward to explain Superman's ability to fly
(even through outer space, where logically he should die from lack of
oxygen), his X-ray vision or his unbelievable strength, we know it's
all hokey. It simply can't happen: Elementary physics tells us that. Yet
we lap it up without a second thought, scientific or Christian. Never
mind the quasi-religious elements: that Superman's name, *Kal El*,
means "like God" in Hebrew, or that the name of his home planet,
Krypton, is Greek for something "hidden" or "secret." We see it for
what it genuinely *is*: a bit of fun to be had by imagining a state of af-
fairs that could never actually exist. Harry Potter's magical world is

the same. To be sure, we might have some justifiable misgivings about the phenomenon of magic used in the series. However, these have nothing to do with the baseless charge of demonism or occultism leveled by many of Harry's critics.

THE DEEPER MAGIC

In fact the kind of magic, wizardry and witchcraft we encounter in Potterworld is very similar to the kind we encounter in another classic work of children's literature, C. S. Lewis's Narnia series. In their time, *The Lion, the Witch and the Wardrobe* and the other six Narnia books were so groundbreaking that they were attacked for being "juvenile" and considerably beneath the undoubted talents of their respected and august creator. Today, though we might criticize them for being rather quaint and for suffering from the kind of flaws that belong to anything that stands as the first in its field, we can hardly attack them for being juvenile.

Still less, however, can we attack them as "demonic creations" in the way that Harry Potter is sometimes attacked. In part this is because they are so well established as part of the canon of children's literature. Many generations have grown up loving Lewis's creations. They are familiar, faithful and foundational to most people in Britain, who have either read them to their children, read them to themselves, or had them read to them by their parents some time in the last fifty years. There is, however, a second and perhaps more compelling reason why the Narnia Chronicles have escaped the kind of criticism and vitriol that has been leveled at Harry Potter: They were written by a man whose Christian credentials were impeccable. Lewis is, in a word, fireproof.

An Oxford don and subsequently Cambridge Professor of Medieval and Renaissance Literature, C. S. Lewis was also, from the late 1930s until his death in 1963, the most respected and skillful defender of Christian orthodoxy in Britain. *Mere Christianity*, a collection of his popular World War II radio broadcasts about the Christian faith, is still almost as influential as it was when it was first published in 1952, and his argument as to why Jesus *cannot* have been merely a "great moral teacher"—but must instead have been either a self-deceiving "lunatic," a self-promoting "fiend" or "God in human form"—continues to form the basis of many evangelistic talks on the identity of Jesus up and down the country, and to some extent across the world. *The Screwtape Letters*—ostensibly written by a senior devil to a junior one, advising him on the best ways to tempt humans to sin—is a profound, satirical and very funny examination of human nature and spirituality, and besides being something of a set-text for would-be "spin doctors," it is one of the very few Christian books frequently read by those who want nothing whatsoever to do with the Church.

The Lion, the Witch and the Wardrobe, the best known of "Jack" Lewis's ten novels,[16] is a classic work of Christian allegory (though the blatantly allegorical elements are generally lost on its millions of young readers). It combines a deceptively simple narrative style with what are now stock-in-trade elements in fantasy children's literature—a sympathetic group of children, an old and unusual house to explore, a mysterious cupboard leading to other realms, magical creatures, a wicked witch, deception, betrayal, outstanding bravery and the eventual triumph of good over evil. It is a benchmark of children's fiction, a book that has stirred hearts and sparked imaginations for over half a century.

It is also filled to the brim with magic. Aslan may not dispense magic from the end of a wand as the evil White Witch does—and as the characters in Potterworld do—but that doesn't make him any less a magical creature. In fact Lewis makes no bones about the fact that magic is a dominant feature in the world of Narnia, sewn into its very fabric by "the Emperor" at "the very beginning," capable of being used for good or for ill. The Witch invokes "Deep Magic" when she points out that Edmund's treachery makes his lifeblood *her* property, and Aslan submits to this when he proposes to die in Edmund's place. He admits and endorses the role that magic plays in Narnia even if he opposes the Witch's malevolent use of it. The idea that he should "work against the Emperor's Magic" is one that he finds unthinkable. But he in turn invokes "deeper magic" when he rises from the dead. Lucy and Susan hear a deafening noise, "a great cracking" and return to the scene of Aslan's death to find the Stone Table broken in two and Aslan's body nowhere to be found. Like the women at Jesus' tomb on the morning of his resurrection, they're totally bewildered.

> *"Who's done it?" cried Susan. "What does it mean? Is it more magic?"*
> *"Yes!" said a great voice behind their backs. "It is more magic . . . Though the Witch knew the Deep Magic, there is a deeper magic still which she did not know."*[17]

Lewis seems to have had no problem with the forces of good and the forces of evil in Narnia using the same basic order of magic. The difference is not that one is "witchcraft and wizardry" and the other is somehow benign, but that one is used for evil and the other is used for good. The heroes of Narnia may not be called witches and wizards or go around waving magic wands but they are very like the heroes of Potterworld in that they use an essentially neutral force—or perhaps even a force designed for good ("the Emperor's Magic") but which has been twisted and used for evil by the stories villains—in order to better the world around them and ensure that right ultimately triumphs over wrong.

Much the same thinking underlies another undisputed literary classic by another safely Christian author, J. R. R. Tolkien. *The Lord of the Rings*, published in three volumes in 1954 and 1955 (contemporaneous with Narnia books five and six), is much darker, more violent and more impregnated with magic and wizardry than the Narnia Chronicles. Nevertheless, in poll after poll, English-language readers have voted it the "best book of the twentieth century"—it is an acknowledged literary masterpiece by a true literary master, unparalleled both in the complexity of its creation and in the sheer amount of background work done by its creator (some published posthumously as *The Silmarillion*, some reedited by Tolkien's son Christopher in his twelve-volume series, *The History of Middle-earth*).

Ronald Tolkien received a great deal of encouragement to write *The Lord of the Rings* from his close friend Jack Lewis, whom he had met (and steered toward the Christian faith) in the early 1930s when he was Professor of Anglo-Saxon at Oxford. The two of them had been part of a small writers' group called "The Inklings." Lewis can hardly have been blind to the magical ingredients of *The Lord of the Rings*. It is, in many ways, a sequel to Tolkien's 1937 bestseller *The Hobbit*, which contains many of the same characters and characteristics. What is more, Lewis had already written repeatedly in praise of Tolkien's 1939 lecture and essay "On Fairy-Stories." Having faced criticism for writing about magical creatures, "Tollers" (as Lewis affectionately called him) had been keen to establish the academic credentials of fairy stories, which he defined as requiring the twin ingredients of humans and the *Faërie* realm. This, he argued, "may perhaps most nearly be translated by Magic."[18] For both Tolkien and

C. S. Lewis, therefore, magic was more than just an accidental ingredient in their work—it was a basic necessity of the genre of story they had chosen to write.

The magic and wizardry of *The Lord of the Rings* is, of course, far more sophisticated than that of Narnia, and the characters, sketched in considerably more detail, are far more nuanced and realistic. The tension between goodness and evil is seen both between and within characters in a way never achieved (or perhaps intended) in Narnia, in part because Lewis was writing far more self-consciously for children. Though there is some suggestion by Tolkien that magic in and of itself can be dangerous and harmful—both Bilbo and Frodo Baggins find themselves warped by possession of the magical One Ring, taking on more and more of the undesirable characteristics of its onetime owner Gollum—the book's basic philosophy seems in many ways to be that magic is an essentially neutral force. The right use of magic enhances a person's innate goodness, while the wrong use exacerbates their innate evil.

It is not just that good people use magic to do good and evil people use it to do evil; there is in *The Lord of the Rings* a recognition that magic is a form of power, and as Lord Acton noted, "power tends to corrupt." When power is used wisely, everyone benefits; when it is used unwisely, all but a few suffer. In the same way, when magic is used wisely, everyone benefits; when it is used unwisely, all but a few suffer. Nevertheless, the temptation to do evil and the possibility of redemption are always there: Saruman, once the greatest of all wizards, falls prey to his own corrupting greed and betrays the forces of good, while Gollum in some senses redeems himself by guiding Frodo to Mount Doom.

One way of interpreting magic in Tolkien (and also in Rowling) is therefore to see it as symbolic. It stands for the use of power. It is a metaphor for how human beings exercise power and the susceptibility of human nature to its abuse. The struggles between good and evil in Middle Earth or Potterworld act as parables that make us think about the kind of struggles for power that take place in our own everyday world. Once we realize this, we see that the criticisms thrown against magic in the Harry Potter books are a misreading of its dramatic and literary function, and are consequently misplaced.

"CAN THE DEVIL SPEAK TRUE?"

If we reject Harry Potter, therefore, on the grounds that it endorses wizardry and magic, or has a tone of darkness about it, we will also have to reject, on exactly the same grounds, both *The Lion, the Witch and the Wardrobe* and *The Lord of the Rings*, as well as keeping a rather close eye on certain parts of the Bible just in case children accidentally get the "wrong" idea. We will also have to expunge from the school syllabus such clearly dubious works of English literature as Shakespeare's *Macbeth*, with its three future-predicting witches and undeniably menacing tone. As with Harry Potter, *The Lion, the Witch and the Wardrobe* and *The Lord of the Rings*, magic and wizardry—in this case the witchcraft of the "weird sisters"—is integral to the plot (though *not* the main theme). Without the witches' prediction that the Scottish war hero Macbeth, the Thane of Glamis, will swiftly rise to become first the Thane of Cawdor and then the King of Scotland, he and his less-than-good lady wife would not have hatched the plot to murder Duncan and claim the throne for themselves. But the witches are not the real villains of the piece, however they may sometimes have been painted. They *predict* the future but they don't actually make it a reality. Instead, it is the very *un*magical Lady Macbeth who sells her soul to the devil, inviting murderous spirits to "fill me from the crown to the toe top full of direst cruelty."[19] And it is the very *un*wizardly Macbeth himself who initiates the final disaster by arranging for the murder of his friend Banquo.

In the end, *Macbeth* is not a play about witchcraft, although witchcraft plays a key role. It is about power, greed and guilt, and the ultimate triumph of good over a self-destructive and murderous brand of evil. Shakespeare could have replaced the witches with another plot device, and still have retained the essential components of the story (in a way that Lewis and Tolkien couldn't). However, the story developed in his own mind *with* the witches and he never saw the need to change it, even though he was writing his plays at a time when witch-hunts were both real and fervent, especially over the border in Scotland where *Macbeth* is set. Shakespeare seems to have felt that his audience, drawn from all walks of life (literally from royalty right down to the gutter), was sophisticated enough to follow the story, and draw the intended moral lesson from it (for *Macbeth* is a very moralizing play), without in the process signing up to occult membership. The answer to Banquo's poignant question, "Can the devil speak true?"[20] would in this case appear to be a solid yes.

Much the same can be said about Harry Potter. As Hermione remarks dismissively of her own wizardry, it is nothing but, "Books! And cleverness! There are more important things—friendship and bravery."[21] In the end, Joanne Rowling's books fundamentally are *not* about witchcraft and wizardry, although witchcraft and wizardry play a key role. They are about a gifted, vulnerable boy called Harry; his equally gifted and equally vulnerable friends Ron and Hermione; their respective and variously dysfunctional families; their adventures in and out of school; their friends and enemies; the problems they face growing up; and the decisive role they play in the ultimate triumph of good over evil. Wizardry is important to the stories but they are not *about* wizardry. Magic is an integral part of the plot but if she had chosen to Rowling (like Shakespeare but *not* Lewis or Tolkien) could potentially have found an alternative plot device and still have retained most of the essential components of the story.

This was a point made by the actor and author Stephen Fry—who reads the Potter books for the British audio versions—when he was asked to interview Joanne Rowling for Bloomsbury's website. "In many ways," he remarked, "the stories would hold together even if there were no magic in them, because what people really come away with seems to be the relationships—particularly, obviously, Hermione, Harry and Ron." Rowling agreed. Though the magic was important, it wasn't *all-important*. In fact ironically, her audience seemed to appreciate the magic more when it *didn't* work than when it *did*. "From the reactions I get, particularly from children, it is the characters they care about most," she explained. "They are deeply amused by the magic going wrong and so on but they really deeply care about the characters, particularly the three central characters: Harry, Ron and Hermione."

Sure enough, in each of the four books published so far, it is not the magic or wizardry of the intrepid trio that wins the day. Instead, it is their all-too-human goodness and friendship, teaming up against an evil that frequently proves itself to be self-defeating. In *Sorcerer's Stone*, for example, it is an equal and ultimately self-sacrificial effort by the three friends—Harry's bravery and ingenuity, Ron's chess skills and Hermione's logic—that gets Harry "through the trapdoor" and into the last chamber for his confrontation with Voldemort and Quirrell, and it is Quirrell's greed and Voldemort's hatred that finally undo their plans to acquire the Elixir of Life. In *Chamber of Secrets*, again it is Hermione's knowledge (gained at great personal cost), Ron's courage and Dumbledore's phoenix that enable Harry to confront the image of the young Voldemort inside the chamber, and it is a tooth from Voldemort's own deadly Basilisk that proves to be his downfall.

In *Azkaban* and *Goblet of Fire*, the situation is more complex, both because the books' endings are not as neat and self-contained as the previous two—they hint at far more to come—and because the various ingredients that make the endings possible are added over a longer period of time. What is more, as the three friends slowly become more adept at magic, magical solutions present themselves more easily. Nevertheless, wizardry is never *the* vital ingredient in resolving problems. It never acts as a kind of *deus ex machina*.

In ancient Greek and Roman theater, if a playwright was at a complete loss to know how to draw the threads of his play together into an acceptable ending, he would introduce a god into the script. An actor, clearly masked as the relevant god, would be winched onto the stage by a wooden crane, descending to earth to make things right. The technique smacked of desperation and the term *deus ex machina* ("a god from a machine") is still used to deride any play, book, film or television program that relies on artificial means to solve plot problems—from the arrival of the U.S. Cavalry just in the nick of time to Bobby Ewing's appearance in the shower to reveal that an entire series of *Dallas* was nothing but a dream! Harry Potter is mercifully free from this kind of device. The solutions that arise are carefully drawn not only from the ingredients of the plot but also from the personalities of the characters involved.

Hermione's time traveling, for example—a literary device not necessarily linked to magic, used to very good effect by Dickens in his fiercely moralistic tale *A Christmas Carol*—is introduced in a veiled way quite early on in *Azkaban* for reasons that fit perfectly with her character as a chronic overachiever. It is her bookishness and enthusiasm that lead to its being a credible factor in the story, and from there the means by which Harry finds the confidence and strength to confront the Dementors. Similarly, in *Goblet of Fire*, when the wand-blasts of Harry's and Voldemort's spells connect in midair, it is the song of Dumbledore's phoenix and the ghostly echoes of Voldemort's victims—Cedric Diggory, Frank Bryce, Bertha Jorkins and Harry's own parents—that give Harry the courage and time to escape death at Voldemort's hands. The magic is there but it is actually the humanity of the characters that proves to be the decisive factor in enabling good to defeat the purposes of evil.

In this, Harry Potter is very similar to television shows like *Bewitched* in the 1960s, or *Sabrina the Teenage Witch* in the 1990s— programs that have equally been accused of promoting the occult. Both of these were long running series, for the reason that they relied on character development rather than the *deus ex machina* of witchcraft and magic. *Bewitched* was essentially about life as an American family: an advertising executive, his work, his wife, his daughter and, of course, his mother-in-law. *Sabrina the Teenage Witch* is essentially about life as an American teenager: a girl, her relatives (two maiden aunts), her school, her friends, her romances and, of course, her talking cat! When we consider shows like these, two things quickly stand out: firstly, the magic is preeminently a *comic* device. Its purpose is to elicit laughter, to make the viewer see the situation from a comedic perspective. Harry Potter is the same: Magical happenings run through every chapter and a large part of their function is to play a joke on the reader. It is as if Joanne Rowling is saying to us: "O come on! Surely you don't take this stuff seriously?" If we fail to recognize the essential playfulness of Potterworld and magic's playful role in it, we shall have misread the series entirely. It can only be understood with a sense of humor.

Second, *Bewitched* and *Sabrina* depend for their longevity on the ability of viewers to identify with the characters. Real wizardry and witchcraft might fill a dozen programs but can't stretch to four or five series—for that you need properly human characters, commonly human problems and essentially human solutions. The same is true of

Harry Potter—the books succeed not because they contain witchcraft and magic but because they contain characters that readers can identify with and care about.

Perhaps that's why Christians have been among both Potterworld's fiercest critics and also its staunchest supporters. For all those—like the reactionary parents in North Carolina—who have insisted with Banquo that "to win us to our harm, the instruments of darkness tell us truths, win us with honest trifles, to betray 's in deepest consequence,"[22] there have been others who have seen far more than "honest trifles" in Harry Potter.

"Children will not find in Harry Potter a tract for the dark arts, but will encounter a world where material and spiritual forces are interwoven," wrote Canon June Osborne in *The Times* (London). "As in most mythical tales, this is a moral and ordered world telling us abiding truths about the human story." Though she sympathized with those who were concerned about exposing children to the occult, Osborne insisted that Harry Potter didn't fall into that category.

> *The strongest message at the heart of these stories is the all-conquering power of love. Harry owes his life, and evil its downfall, to an act of self-sacrifice. How that love infiltrates Harry's life is a positive influence on our children's scheme of values. Christians and many others will recognise such themes and doubly rejoice: that they are being told to our children as well as being so much enjoyed.*[23]

So is Harry Potter a demonic creation? I firmly believe not. Though the books contain witchcraft and evil, they don't promote these things any more than *The Lion, the Witch and the Wardrobe* or *The Lord of the Rings*, which also contain witchcraft and evil. In fact in many ways the Potter books are *less* linked to magic and wizardry than the very *un*demonic works of Lewis and Tolkien. Is Harry

Potter a daredevil hero? Again, I believe not. As we'll see in Chapter Two, he's not Superboy. He may be courageous and skilled on the Quidditch pitch but he's far from omnipotent. There's a fundamental realism to him, a vulnerability, without which he would never have appealed to both children and adults in the way he has. At the end of the day, Harry is neither devil nor saint—he's essentially "the boy who lived."

chapter two

THE MIRROR OF ERISED

THE ATTRACTION
OF POTTERWORLD

*He'll be famous—a legend—I wouldn't be
surprised if today was known as Harry Potter Day
in future—there will be books written about
Harry—every child in our world will know his
name!*[1]

Harry Potter is, of course, a literary phenomenon.

From a very modest initial print run of just five hundred hardback copies of *Sorcerer's Stone* in June 1997, Pottermania has taken the world completely by storm. The books have been translated into over forty languages; selling around forty million copies and winning many literary awards in Britain and elsewhere (including the Nestlé Smarties Gold Medal in the nine- to eleven-year-old category three years running, and the highly prestigious Whitbread Children's Book of the Year for 1999). J. K. Rowling has gone from being so poor that she had to scribble the first book in cafés because she couldn't afford to heat her small flat, to being one of the highest-paid authors in the world, listed among the top twenty-five "celebrity high-earners" in the fashion-conscious *Forbes* magazine. Meanwhile Harry himself is almost as universally known and talked about in the real Muggle world as he is among the witches and wizards of the books.

No one—not the British publisher Bloomsbury, nor her agent Christopher Little, and least of all Rowling herself—predicted the astonishing scale of Harry's success. In fact Bloomsbury's decision to publish *Sorcerer's Stone* using Rowling's initials, J. K., instead of her first name, Joanne, was prompted by their lack of confidence that ten-year-old boys would buy a magical adventure story written by a woman, and their equal uncertainty that ten-year-old girls would buy a magical adventure story whose hero was a boy. The whole thing could so easily have been a recipe for disaster instead of the recipe for runaway success that it has been. Rowling agreed to having her initials used because she was pleased and grateful just to have her work actually published and earning her a tiny bit of money. (As she joked to Stephen Fry, "I would have called myself Enid Snodgrass had they so required!") In the nine months or so between Bloomsbury's acceptance of *Sorcerer's Stone* and its release on the market, as well as in the first few months of sales (before word of mouth made it catch on), she lived on her lowly royalty advance of roughly $2500 (average for a non-bestselling novel) and a grant of about $10,000 from the Scottish Arts Council (which seems to value children's literature). She used the money to buy her own computer (and, we can only assume, heat her flat) in order to finish the second installment in the Potter saga, *Chamber of Secrets*. There was nothing of a bidding war—profit-hungry publishers offering six- or seven-figure advances for what they consider surefire winners—of the kind that has often accompanied less deserving novels. Bloomsbury took a genuine risk in giving the world Harry Potter—a risk that has, of course, paid off very handsomely for all concerned.

But just what *is* it that has caught on? Why has Harry Potter sold in its millions? Why has it successfully translated into so many languages, inspiring children and adults alike from cultures as diverse as Britain, France, Germany, Iceland, Serbia, Russia, America, Japan and China? What is the irresistible attraction of Potterworld? And what does its success suggest about the role of imagination in religion and literature?

RESPECT

The phenomenal popularity of the Potter books owes a considerable amount to certain key things: Rowling's indisputable skill as a storyteller; the basic cohesiveness of Potterworld as a literary creation; the magical atmosphere pervading both Hogwarts and the books in general; the gradual development of the central characters; the intelligent use of human archetypes; the cleverness of the various plot devices; the inventiveness of the different secondary elements (such as the sweets or the text book titles); and the essential humor of Potterworld.

As far as their appeal to children is concerned, the thing that soon becomes most apparent is that they relate to them on *their* level. The books are, as various critics, reviewers and parents have noted, free from condescension. Rowling never talks down to her younger readers. In this she has been compared to the established figures of children's literature like Lewis Carroll, Kenneth Grahame, A. A. Milne, C. S. Lewis, J. R. R. Tolkien and Roald Dahl. The compliments and comparisons are, I think, well deserved. But what is truly remarkable is not the fact that Joanne Rowling *doesn't* write down to children but the implicit assumption that *any* decent children's author *does*. To say that Rowling has respect for children is to say that an author has respect for her readers; and that is an essential quality in *all* good fiction writing, whether it is aimed at children or not.

In fact in many ways, Rowling is not writing for children at all. Aware, no doubt, that Carroll, Grahame, Milne, Tolkien and the creator of Peter Pan, J. M. Barrie, all wrote their children's classics from stories each had told to specific individual children, journalists have continually asked Rowling whether she writes Harry Potter with her daughter, Jessica, in mind. In reply, she has pointed out that she started writing before Jessica was even born and that she doesn't write with *anyone* particular in mind. While she is careful to write in a way that is accessible to children—a harder task than writing purely for adults—she writes largely to please herself. Asked what would happen after book seven, she suggested that she would continue to write but not about Harry Potter and perhaps not even for children. Like all of the aforementioned literary greats (with the possible exception of Grahame), she seems to perceive herself as an *author* rather than as a dedicated *children's author*. The Potter stories are children's stories not because she particularly wants to write for children but because Harry and his friends are children; and because the storylines and main characters burst into Rowling's imagination *as children's stories*. She doesn't appear to have had to shape them as such—that was the form they came in to begin with.

C. S. Lewis would have been proud. He had no time for those critics and authors who felt that the way to write a successful children's story was to work out "what children want" and then simply give it to them. In his 1952 lecture "On Three Ways of Writing for Children," delivered to the Library Association, he explained how a woman had sent him the manuscript of a book she had written involving a machine which could give a child whatever they wanted at the flick of a switch or press of a button. Lewis replied that he "didn't much care for that sort of thing." The woman, in turn, admitted that she didn't really like it either, "But it is what the modern child wants."[2] Similarly, Lewis told the Library Association, a father had once suggested that he had written the chapter in *The Lion, the Witch and the Wardrobe* in which Mr. Tumnus the Faun invites Lucy to tea because he had calculated that children would enjoy reading about a feast. In fact, Lewis revealed, he had written the scene because *he* enjoyed reading about a feast—he had done so as a child and, in his fifties, still did.

In much the same way Rowling's descriptions of the lavish, magical Hogwarts feasts or the various cakes and sweets (Cauldron Cakes, Chocolate Frogs, Licorice Wands, Bertie Bott's Every Flavor Beans, Droobles Best Blowing Gum and, of course, foaming tankards of hot Butterbeer) available to wizards don't appear to have come from a conscious desire to give children what they want. It is not just children who like the sound of Butterbeer or fancy taking a risk with an Every Flavor Bean. In fact adults far more than children appreciate the idea of a feast that appears magically out of thin air, cooked to perfection, and then disappears afterward without any need for washing up . . . or a fridge full of leftovers! As with so much of Potterworld, what appeals to child readers is identical to what appeals to adult readers.

Rowling and Lewis, then, belong to Lewis's third way of writing for children: Their creations stem directly from their imaginations, created not to pander to children's supposed literary desires or even to amuse a specific child but as a natural form of expression for the author's creative instincts. In devising Potterworld, Rowling has given us what *she* wants to read, not what she thinks *we*—or our children—want to read. Her only concession to children is that she has written her stories in a way that *includes* rather than *excludes* them.

This contrasts with an underlying assumption that what children like in stories and what adults like are distinct spheres with little common ground. In fact this is not true. Children aren't a "breed apart," unfathomable in their tastes and entirely unrelated to the adult world in terms of what they like to read, watch or listen to. I am aware, of course, that this may sound incredible to any parent who has had to endure an episode of *Pokémon* or read the same Dr. Seuss story twenty-six times to their toddler—which is probably most of us. However, it is important to point out that it is not actually the *content* of *Pokémon* or Dr. Seuss stories that we tend to object to but the *lack* of content. Because children's intellectual and emotional capacities develop only gradually, the kind of stories and characters that appeal to them are initially simple ones. There is no plot in *Spot*, for example, nor much character development in *Teletubbies*. But as they get older, children become able to understand and appreciate more and more of the elements that make up a good story: plot, sympathetic character development, ideas, atmosphere, surprise or suspense, action, intrigue, humor and space for imagination. The basic difference between a book written especially for children and one written for adults is that a children's book will contain fewer of these elements and they will be expressed in far simpler and more accessible terms geared to the right level of understanding and ignorance.

In other words, children don't so much "trade in" their likes and dislikes for adult ones when they reach the age of majority as "trade up." They *add* to their tastes and abilities rather than straightforwardly *replace* them. Much the same is true with music. Those who grow up listening to jazz or rock will *continue* listening to jazz or rock, though they may slowly lose patience with less rewarding examples of the genre and broaden their tastes to include other musical styles. In the same way, those children who develop an early taste for adventure stories will probably retain that interest, though they will hopefully graduate from the simple stories and characters of Enid Blyton's Famous Five to the greater intricacy of thrillers by Alistair MacLean, Tom Clancy, P. D. James or John Grisham (or perhaps the work of such nineteenth-century "potboiler" writers as Charles Dickens, Alexandre Dumas or Robert Louis Stevenson). Conversely, those who don't like fantasy or science fiction when they are ten are unlikely to develop a taste for it as adults, even if it comes from the pen of such established literary giants as Jules Verne, H. G. Wells, Aldous Huxley, George Orwell or J. R. R. Tolkien. Our taste as children is generally a simplified and narrower version of our taste as adults. As C. S. Lewis explained:

> *We must write for children out of those elements in our own imagination which we share with children; differing from our child readers not by any less, or less serious, interest in the things we handle, but by the fact that we have other interests which children would not share with us.*[3]

So those children who actually *don't like* Harry Potter—and they exist, though they are probably in hiding—aren't exhibiting precocious maturity any more than those adults who *do like* Harry Potter are exhibiting childish or recidivist tendencies. It isn't the *child* in us that responds to Potterworld—it's the *person*. The stories aren't ones that appeal to "children of all ages," from seven to seventy; they are ones that appeal to *people* of all ages, from seven to seventy. As Lewis said in defense of Tolkien's *The Hobbit*, "This is a children's book only in the sense that the first of many readings can be undertaken in the nursery."[4] Two years later, Tolkien defended himself in a similar vein: "If fairy-story as a kind is worth reading at all it is worthy to be written for and read by adults. They will, of course, put more in and get more out than children can."[5] Either of these comments could equally apply to Harry Potter.

"THE NAME'S POTTER . . . HARRY POTTER."

Some of the details in Potterworld, of course, *do* seem to be aimed especially (though by no means exclusively) at child readers: Pepper Imps, Ice Mice or Cockroach Clusters, for example, have more appeal to children than adults, as do Dungbombs, Bubotuber pus, Dr. Filibuster's Fabulous No-Heat, Wet-Start Fireworks and, of course, the ever-popular Quidditch (though I have to confess that my favorites are the Every Flavor Beans). Some details, by contrast, are obviously more intended to appeal to older readers: The fact that Madam Maxime's horses drink only single malt whiskey, for instance, or that human-looking mandrakes are fully mature "the moment they start trying to move into each other's pots,"[6] will be funny but not *entirely* comprehensible to children. Like the blatant references to the atonement in Lewis's *The Lion, the Witch and the Wardrobe* or the hookah (a water-filtered pipe used for smoking marijuana as well as tobacco) in Carroll's *Alice's Adventures in Wonderland*, these kinds of detail generally pass over the heads of child readers, who accept them at face value without understanding the full adult implications.

The vast majority of the details and ideas used in Potterworld, however, are ones that appeal right across the age range: Socks that scream loudly when they become too smelly or the sight of tiny Professor Flitwick sailing through the air as a result of Neville Longbottom's badly aimed Banishing Charm. The appeal of Potterworld, in other words, is essentially the same for all ages who respond to the same basic qualities. The rest of this chapter is devoted to discussing what these are. Just for the sake of convenience, I will break them down into two distinct groups: *primary* qualities, related to the basic story being told, and *secondary* qualities, concerned with the atmospheric details of Potterworld itself. However, this is not an indication of importance. Both primary and secondary qualities are essential components in Harry Potter's success. Without the primary qualities, there is no real story to tell; without the secondary qualities, the story would never grip the imagination in the phenomenal way it does.

The main story in Harry Potter is an old one and the most basic available: nothing less than good versus evil. Though an in-depth discussion of the morality of Potterworld will have to wait until the next chapter, it is important to note at this point that the Harry Potter stories are, at heart, *moral* tales. They are not merely concerned with a young boy's progress through and adventures in an eccentric boarding school, though that established literary genre (dating at least back to Dickens) is certainly present in large amounts. Nor are they just tales about a hero with extraordinary skills, though that literary genre (dating right back to the ancient Greek myths of men like Hercules) is there, too. Instead, the stories' canvas is much greater, and takes in the eternal epic fight between the forces of good, in the person of Harry and his friends, and the forces of evil, represented by the Dark Lord, Voldemort.

This is, of course, a very ambitious project; and it remains to be seen if Rowling will succeed in her efforts to achieve it. The fact that she has succeeded so far is no guarantee of future glory—other, equally talented writers have fallen at the last fence. There is, for example, a sense in which the later six Narnia books, in attempting to expand the story beyond the tight confines of *The Lion, the Witch and the Wardrobe*, actually diminish its scope and power. Something is lost in the upgrading of scale between the allegorical fable of *Lion* and the near-epic pretensions of the expanded Narnia saga. It is extraordinarily difficult to capture the scope of an epic on the pages of a book, and Lewis only partially succeeds.

In fact very few writers have managed to create a real epic on the page, and those who have succeeded have generally done so by concentrating on just a handful of key players. In his seminal poem *The Iliad*, for example, Homer truncates his telling of the entire ten-year Trojan War into its final and decisive year, and not even this is related in its entirety. The ending of the siege, with its defeat of Troy through the famous Wooden Horse, isn't revealed until his "sequel" volume, *The Odyssey*. Both works also have a generous use of "flashback" in an effort to contain the action and keep the scale of the story manageable. A slightly different approach, though one again anchored in just a few central characters, is seen in Tolkien's *The Lord of the Rings*. Here the journey undertaken by Frodo, and the conflicts that accompany it, are essentially just the endgame in the epic battle between good and evil more hinted at than described through the narrow window of the novel.

The key to handling an epic, in other words, is never to show more than a slice of it at any one time and never to let it overwhelm the credibility of the main characters. Though she already knows what will happen in Harry's remaining years at Hogwarts, this is the challenge facing Rowling in the final books—to find a way to present the showdown between good and evil without losing her focus on the essentially human elements of Harry and his friends. The conflict between Voldemort and Harry, between good and evil, elevates the story above mere boarding school fiction or witch and wizardly to a point where it connects with something elemental in the human spirit. The full cosmic drama of the eternal conflict between good and evil is encapsulated in the adventures of a single boy. But without the firm grounding of that boy's very real strengths and weaknesses, and the limitations of his environment, the story loses its tether to identifiable, sympathetic characters.

When that happens, of course, things inevitably end up going the way of so many James Bond films, where million-dollar stunts take the place of a credible story and crassness takes the place of genuine characters. It is no coincidence that the best Bond films, such as *From Russia with Love*, concentrate the action and focus on the central characters, while the worst, such as *Moonraker*, abandon all attempts at a plausible story in favor of cartoon villains bent on world domination, and big-budget action scenes. The best stand as films in their own right; the worst rely on their 007 branding and an industrial-strength pinch of salt.

So while the showdown with Voldemort takes Potterworld to the threshold of epic, it is the concreteness of Harry's everyday world that sustains the appeal. Without the mundane reality of lessons and exams, Harry's arguments with Ron and Hermione (and their arguments with, and attraction to, each other), and his run-ins with Malfoy and the ambiguous Snape, the richness of Potterworld—and our ability to identify with it—would be seriously diminished. It is these, after all, which stop the special effects running away with the story. If they are to avoid becoming nothing more than the literary equivalent of "eye candy," the Potter books will have to keep their more epic elements on a tight leash. Rather than letting herself over-inflate the series into apocalyptic, Rowling will have to ensure that Harry's part in the battle between good and evil never grows beyond his carefully drawn limitations. If she fails in this, however grand the scale of things, she will have no tale to tell. That she knows this is clear from her interview with Stephen Fry. "The most important thing, when you're creating a fantasy world, is to set the rules," she told him. "You have to decide, first of all, most importantly, what [your characters] *can't* do, way before you decide what they *can* do. Otherwise you actually have no story at all." Perhaps this is why the stories have so far been mostly contained within the bounds of Hogwarts School.

WINGED BOARS

Hogwarts represents far more in Potterworld than just an eccentric educational establishment. It represents far more, too, than just the stage on which the stories are set. It is, in a sense, the place where "heaven" meets "earth," where the magical meets the mundane. Once pupils pass in (literal) horseless carriages through its hallowed gates, "flanked with statues of winged boars,"[7] toward the towers of the craggy castle, they have entered an environment which mirrors almost everything else in Potterworld. On the one hand, it is here that most of the magical action takes place—where, in some form or another (even in *Goblet of Fire*, where a Portkey transports Harry miles away to the Riddle family graveyard), Harry and his friends do battle with the forces of evil. On the other hand, it is in Hogwarts (rather than in the Muggle world of the Dursleys) that Harry encounters what, for him at least, passes for "normality." And it is in the interaction between these two spheres, the magical and the mundane, that we find most of the primary qualities that attract us to Potterworld.

Many of the magical aspects of the school will be discussed elsewhere, either because they function as what I call "secondary" qualities in their own right or because they contribute to our understanding of the moral, theological or metaphysical elements of Potterworld. For the moment, we need merely note the role the school plays in the gradually unfolding story. In part, Hogwarts acts as a surrogate family environment for Harry Potter, even more than usual for a boarding school. It is here that Harry lives for (the happiest) ten months of the year, here that he learns and grows as a boy, and here that he receives love, support and guidance from both friends and staff. However, because it is a magical place, Hogwarts also functions as the traditional (but extremely varied) "wonderland" of this basic genre of children's story—like the Wonderland and Looking Glass worlds of Lewis Carroll, the Neverland of J. M. Barrie, the Hundred Acre Wood of A. A. Milne, the Narnia of C. S. Lewis, the Midnight Garden of Philippa Pearce, the Chocolate Factory of Roald Dahl and the parallel universes of Philip Pullman. In Hogwarts, the land of anything-is-possible and the land of clean-out-your-room converge into one double-value dramatic location: home and away. It is both the mysterious castle in which strange and exciting adventures happen and the stable setting to which Harry, at least, returns for a dose of normality and ordinariness after the adventures are over.

As strange as it may seem, given that the books recount the adventures of a young wizard, ordinariness is one of the touchstones of Harry Potter's phenomenal success, and it is Hogwarts that allows this to surface. Good stories need good heroes, and Harry is one of the best, but what works about him is not so much his superpowers as his basic humanity. Although he has some sporting ability on the Quidditch pitch, for example, and is far from stupid, Harry is in most ways a very ordinary boy, and Hogwarts helps to underline this.

Were his adventures set mainly in the nonwizarding, Muggle world, Harry would in fact be a far less interesting literary character. His magic would set him apart from everyone else and this magical difference would be the key component in the eventual resolution of all the novels' plots. But as we saw in Chapter One, magic is *not* the key component: character is. Because Harry's adventures are set in Hogwarts, where absolutely *everyone* (except Mr. Filch) practices magic—and where Harry's skill is therefore *average* everywhere but on the Quidditch pitch (where magic plays only an incidental role)—the qualities that make him great, and able to defeat Voldemort, are the kind of essentially *human* qualities that readers share with most of Potterworld's characters. In fact Harry has only one "superpower" above and beyond the skills of an ordinary wizard—his accidental ability to speak Parseltongue—and this actually serves to alienate him rather than elevate him from his peers.

AN UNHOLY TRINITY

Harry, in other words, is very much like the rest of us. He is vulnerable and limited. He needs glasses to see (matron Madam Pomfrey, who can make limbs regrow overnight, is seemingly either unable or unwilling to correct his eyesight), and whatever he tries to do with his unruly hair it never seems to be entirely presentable. We first encounter him as a baby too young to fend for himself, and find him next living in "the Cupboard under the Stairs" in the Dursley house in Privet Drive, frequently bullied by the bigger and far stupider Dudley. From these inauspicious beginnings a real hero is fashioned, but this happens as much by circumstance as anything else. Even Harry's fame among fellow wizards stems from something for which he is not, and does not feel, knowingly responsible: He is merely "the boy who lived."

Harry's main quality, for example—his courage (something Rowling has admitted she finds the most admirable human attribute)—is something he has in great abundance but not something that's unique to him. In *Sorcerer's Stone*, the patched, frayed, dirty old Sorting Hat chooses him for Gryffindor, a house renowned for prizing courage high above all other qualities. Endowed by Hogwarts' four founders with the ability to perceive the appropriate characteristics for each house, the Sorting Hat assigns students on the basis of the quality they most exhibit: The *cleverest* are chosen for Ravenclaw, the *hardest-working* for Hufflepuff, the *most ambitious* for Slytherin and the *bravest* for Gryffindor. In other words, Harry shares his core quality with absolutely *everyone* in his house, including (for reasons that are only just beginning to become clear) the unfortunate Neville Longbottom.

In particular, he shares the quality of courage with his best friends Ron and Hermione. (Despite Hermione's legendary workaholism and intelligence, the Hat sorts her for Gryffindor rather than Hufflepuff or Ravenclaw—a fact we could simply chalk down to the author's need to keep Potterworld's trinity together if it weren't for the fact that Hermione undoubtedly *does* exhibit a great deal of courage.) All three venture through the trapdoor in *Sorcerer's Stone*, and it takes no less courage for Ron and Hermione to sacrifice themselves than it does for Harry to continue on to the last chamber to confront Voldemort and Quirrell. If Hermione isn't there to brave the eight-legged horrors of the Forbidden Forest in *Chamber of Secrets*, it is only because she has already been courageous enough to confirm her suspicions about the basilisk, and is petrified on her way to warn Harry and Ron; Ron, similarly, is held back from the dénouement by a rock slide in the tunnel, not a lack of derring-do. All three brave the first encounter with Sirius Black in *Azkaban*, and with Ron out of action with a broken leg, it is a joint effort from Harry and Hermione that saves Black and Buckbeak from the death penalty. In *Goblet of Fire*, Harry's role as a Triwizard champion means that he has to face

Voldemort alone but even here his courage is bolstered by the echoes of Voldemort's former victims emitted from his wand (in particular, Harry's parents), just as the courage to face Tom Riddle in *Chamber of Secrets* comes in part from the presence of Dumbledore's phoenix, Fawkes.

None of the three main characters, in other words, is perfect. None could achieve what they do without the help and support of the others, and it is these areas of vulnerability that make them not only more credible as characters but sympathetic, too. Despite his tremendous courage, Harry is prone to occasionally crippling self-doubt (and initially wishes there were a fifth house at Hogwarts, for "people who felt a bit queasy").[8] Older readers may well identify with this but young and old alike find themselves urging him on. We don't just sit in admiration of his abilities, we actually *take part* in the story, willing him to succeed. Harry's weaknesses draw us into the story in a way that his strengths never do. They give us a role and effectively put us "on stage." Part of the attraction of Potterworld is the feeling of involvement that comes from identification with Harry in his moment of need. Without this, there is no real identification in his moment of glory.

And it is not just Harry. Hermione, in turn, is a bossy, chronic overachiever. When we first meet her in *Sorcerer's Stone*, the kindness and friendship she shows to Neville is overshadowed by her more irritating characteristics. Nevertheless, by the end of Halloween, we are just as won over as Harry and Ron. "From that moment on," Rowling says, speaking as much for her readers as for her dynamic duo, "Hermione Granger became their friend. There are some things you can't share without ending up liking each other, and knocking out a twelve-foot mountain troll is one of them."[9] We don't become suddenly blind to her failings and irritating habits—quite the opposite. It is these that help make her endearing, especially to older readers aware of their own failings and irritating habits. We know that Rowling is right when she tells us, during Harry and Ron's falling-out, that "there was much less laughter, and a lot more hanging around in the library when Hermione was your best friend,"[10] but we don't mind any more than Harry does. We, like him, accept her as she is, warts and all. The same is true of Ron, whose anger can get the better of him, whose memory can prove to be highly selective, and whose stereotypically male insensitivity stops him, in Hermione's angry words, from having "spotted I'm a girl."[11] Rather than putting us off, these very human weaknesses help us to identify with the central characters, appreciating all the more their very human strengths. They under*line* rather than under*mine* their developing greatness.

Only "achieved" greatness is *true* greatness; and it is one of the primary qualities of Potterworld—one of its appeals—that we see this greatness gradually developing. Its presence elevates the Potter stories above boarding school or witch tales to connect with something basic and important in human nature. At the same time, the fact that it is achieved gradually, amid all-too-human frailty and failings, makes it not just credible but dramatically interesting. The best stories tell us something about who we really are, especially in relation to the eternal battle (in all its various guises) between good and evil; but they do so by giving us characters we can identify with, understand and support. The primary qualities that appeal to us about Potterworld, therefore, are those that connect together the epic with the human. They give us a set of realistic heroes we can believe in amid all the ups and downs of a battle we recognize is genuinely worth fighting, and one in which we can see that we have some sort of role.

The secondary qualities of Potterworld build on this. In calling them secondary, I'm not trying to suggest that they are any less important in terms of Harry Potter's appeal than the primary qualities. Though it is a major component of the books' critical and commercial success that they have a meaningful story to tell—and real, sympathetic characters through whom to tell it—these *primary* qualities are not what stick most in the mind. When we think of what appeals to us about Potterworld, the qualities we think of are predominantly *secondary* ones—the imaginative details that flesh out the basic story and create the enjoyable atmosphere that makes the stories so readable.

Some stories, of course, actually begin with secondary qualities. J. R. R. Tolkien, for example, spent many years doing "background" work for *The Hobbit* and *The Lord of the Rings* purely for fun before writing even a single word of the final novels. In fact the books might never have been written at all if it weren't for the pressure his friend "Jack" Lewis put on him to turn the detailed mythologies, histories, languages and genealogies he had created for Middle Earth into proper stories. "You know Jack," Tolkien later told Lewis's assistant, Walter Hooper. "He had to have a *story*!"[12] For Tolkien, most of the secondary elements came first, and the primary qualities that made the eventual story so powerful slowly grew out of this painstakingly constructed fantasy world. To a lesser extent, the same was true of Lewis's own creation: Narnia. "*The Lion* all began with a picture of a faun carrying an umbrella and parcels in a snowy wood," he told readers of the *Radio Times* in 1960. "This picture had been in my head since I was about sixteen. Then one day, when I was about 40, I said to myself: 'Let's try to make a story about it.' "[13] In a similar way, Joanne Rowling has suggested that the basic starting point for Harry Potter wasn't a plot or story but a question: What if the magical and fantasy elements were *real*? What if there actually *were* such things as trolls, dragons, leprechauns, goblins, flying broomsticks and magic spells?

For many readers, it is the intricacy and completeness of Potterworld that makes for a genuinely irresistible read. The whole thing is so vividly imaginative and clever that we get caught up in Harry's world, and find that suspending our disbelief—essential for any work of fiction—becomes extremely easy. To borrow an image from the beginning of *Sorcerer's Stone*, the richness and inventiveness in the details of Rowling's creation make the thick pane of glass separating reader and Potterworld vanish. Harry and all his friends escape the narrow confines of the printed page and are let loose in our imaginations.

MOOREEFFOC

As part of the intricacy, virtually everything in the Muggle world has its magical counterpart in wizarding life, from Owl Post and Ordinary Wizarding Levels right through to antiseptic (a smoking purple potion) and alcoholism (house-elf Winky's tragic dependency on Butterbeer). The Department of Magical Transportation insists that wizards need a license to Apparate and that they pass an Apparition Test to qualify. Children ride toy broomsticks that rise no higher than about a foot off the ground and collect cards about famous wizards from the wrappers of Chocolate Frogs. Hogwarts uses substitute teachers when permanent staff are unable to teach and insists on a "uniform" of black school robes (different in color and style from those of other wizarding schools). Witches buy *Witch Weekly* for the recipes or the gossip, while serious news (or irresponsible tabloid-style reporting) is covered by the *Daily Prophet*. Mirrors tell you bluntly how you look (or, in the case of the Mirror of Erised, show you your heart's desire), while family grandfather clocks show where different family members presently are rather than what time it is.

The effect of these inventive magical equivalents of Muggle artifacts and behavior is to reflect our own reality back to us but sufficiently altered that it challenges our perceptions. It is what the prominent early-twentieth-century Christian writer (and Fr. Brown creator) G. K. Chesterton (building on an idea first developed by Charles Dickens) called "*Mooreeffoc*." For Dickens, this was a normal London street seen from an odd angle: the inside of a *coffee room*, looking out through the glass window, reading the sign backward. Chesterton developed this idea as a metaphor for the strangeness that familiar objects can take on when we present them from very unfamiliar angles.[14] This is very much what Rowling does, consciously or not. In the course of presenting us with the imaginative, rich textures of Potterworld, she shines a spotlight on our own everyday reality, as subsequent chapters in this book will demonstrate.

It doesn't really matter that a similar kind of magic/Muggle equivalence has been done before by other novelists, besides Dickens and Chesterton (Terry Pratchett's Discworld books, along with Goscinny and Uderzo's Asterix adventures, are contemporary examples). For while Rowling may not be entirely original in creating detailed and humorous magical equivalents of everyday things, she is nevertheless very inventive and usually makes better use of her creations than her predecessors. Living paintings and animated chess pieces, for example, are both found in Chapter One of Lewis Carroll's 1872 classic, *Through the Looking Glass*—the paintings are nothing but a throwaway line, while the chess pieces recur through the book, as playing cards did in *Alice's Adventures in Wonderland*. In Potterworld, however, although the chess pieces are never more than a minor detail, they don't simply talk—they shout strategic advice: "Don't send me there, can't you see his knight? Send *him*, we can afford to lose *him*."[15] Meanwhile, the idea of living paintings comes into its own. Characters can move from one portrait to another, interacting both with each other and with the Hogwarts students. Sir Cadogan volunteers to guard Gryffindor's Portrait Hole when the Fat Lady is attacked by Sirius Black in *Azkaban*, but fails properly to understand the nature of the job and is sacked when he lets Black back into Gryffindor Tower simply because he has the correct password. Similarly, the Fat Lady herself, we learn in *Goblet of Fire*, once told off the young Molly Weasley for returning at four in the morning after a romantic stroll with fellow student Arthur. The motif is developed further when it comes to photographs which reflect not just someone's appearance but their personality as well: In *Chamber of Secrets*, a black and white Lockhart tries to drag the camera-shy Harry into frame in one of Colin Creevey's snapshots, while in *Goblet of Fire*, Victor Krum appears as reticent in his publicity photos as he is in real life. Rowling's imaginative *use* of these kinds of idea helps to sustain the interest and humor in her books, even when similar ideas have been used by others before.

"AND ON THE SIXTH DAY,
GOD CREATED LITERATURE . . ."

These highly detailed secondary qualities do more than just amuse us—they also spark our creative imaginations. There can't be many of us who haven't, at some point, wanted to fly on a broomstick (or even one of Ali Bashir's carpets), Apparate or travel by Floo powder.

By vividly imagining things we *can't* do, we come to see not only the limits of the things we *can* do but also ways of stretching those limits. The idea of the flying broomstick or magic carpet, for example, predates by centuries the first, twelve-second-long, 120-foot powered flight by Orville Wright in December 1903. But without that vision, nurtured by literature, it is doubtful that the Wright brothers would ever have built the world's first working airplane. H. G. Wells' 1901 classic, *The First Men in the Moon*, also significantly predated the manned space flight programs, providing an imaginative spur to their designers. In the same way, the inventive magical details of Potterworld allow us to explore the limits of our own world and provide our imaginations with the stimulus needed to push out the boundaries of those limitations as far as they will go. As odd as it seems, the magical Potterworld may well help to create a new generation of visionaries—from scientists and inventors to teachers and peacemakers.

And it is not just in practical ways that our imaginations are pushed to be more creative: There is something authentically *spiritual* about using our imaginations in this way. Tolkien believed that creating and inhabiting literary worlds was essentially a form of "subcreation"—a genuinely spiritual and religious discipline. Defending Middle Earth against its detractors, who felt that it was nothing but childish fantasy, he wrote: "Fantasy remains a human right: we make in our measure and in our derivative mode, because we are made: and not only made but made in the image and likeness of a Maker."[16] There is, he felt, something about creating or inhabiting what he called a "Secondary World," through the medium of writing and reading literature, that links us directly with our identity as created beings made in the image of a Creator God.

For one thing, as *"Mooreeffoc,"* it gives us a new perspective on and respect for the everyday "Primary World" we live in:

> *Fantasy is made out of the Primary World, but a good craftsman loves his*
> *material, and has a knowledge and feeling for clay, stone and wood which*
> *only the art of making can give. By the forging of Gram cold iron was re-*
> *vealed; by the making of Pegasus horses were ennobled.*[17]

In the course of enjoying literary worlds and creatures, and being challenged by them, we develop a better appreciation for the world and creatures that *God* has made.

For Tolkien, the actual act of creating a Secondary World made this link with God even stronger—those who made literary worlds were "sub-creators," fulfilling their destiny as beings made in the Creator's image and sharing in the process and task of creation. Tolkien's imaginary world was immensely complex: The detail of the creation of Middle Earth is simply astonishing. Tolkien clearly took his role as sub-creator seriously. By comparison, Potterworld and almost every other literary world is a mere sketch. Nevertheless, Middle Earth aside, Potterworld is a remarkably complex and complete world. Rowling, whether she believes in a Creator God or not, is nonetheless honoring him in the act of sub-creating so inventive and detailed a world.

It is this inspired use of imagination, moreover, that enables us to make a further positive assessment of Rowling's achievement. In a vivid phrase redolent of Picasso, the Christian writer Leland Ryken calls literature "the lie that tells the truth."[18] All literature, all fictive worlds (he argues) are deliberate constructions. They are not realistic in the sense that they give us snapshots of the "real" world. They are make-believe. They simplify and heighten reality. They are fantasies. But for all this they tell the truth about human nature and about the things that really matter to us. To step into an alternative world is un-real but it is at the same time truthful. As he puts it, "Despite all its far-flung fantasies, however, the artistic imagination is a window to reality. The imagination transforms the materials it takes from everyday life but by means of that transformation we are led to see reality more clearly."[19]

Understanding this point is crucial if we are to arrive at a fair view of Harry Potter. Even now, there are those Christians who will have nothing to do with imaginary realities on the grounds that they encourage children to believe in lies and distract them from the "real" world; and this surely lies behind some of the hostility toward Harry Potter. But if the thesis put forward by Ryken is correct, the creation of alternate worlds is a *good* thing, for it is in such worlds that we (especially children) can be presented with—and begin to work through—some of the deeper questions of life.[20] To quote Ryken once more:

No matter how unreal some of the conventions of the arts might be, the human issues portrayed are those of actual human experience. Our excursions into the imagined world of the arts are not an escape from reality but a journey into reality.[21]

What is more, Rowling's creativity is growing. With each volume the details of Potterworld become clearer and cleverer. The two short pseudonymous books written in aid of Comic Relief, Newt Scamander's *Fantastic Beasts & Where to Find Them* and Kennilworthy Whisp's *Quidditch Through the Ages*, have continued and expanded the trend by introducing secondary literature on Potterworld by Rowling herself. Though we may never see the publication in the Muggle world of the thousand-plus-page *Hogwarts, A History* (or, as Hermione dubs it, " 'A *Revised* History of Hogwarts' or 'A Highly Biased and *Selective* History of Hogwarts, Which Glosses Over the Nastier Aspects of the School' "),[22] we can still hope to see what I've called the "secondary qualities" of Potterworld developing even more in years to come.

It doesn't matter that this sub-creation is sometimes flawed. We are, after all, flawed and fallen creatures—a fact the media have occasionally attempted to deny in Rowling's case. A blast of publicity surrounded the discovery of a typographical error in the hastily published *Goblet of Fire*,[23] though typos are not unusual even in bestsellers. The media reports, as well as Bloomsbury's rather unconvincing insistence that Rowling herself wasn't to blame for the slip, almost implied that she was "above" such human fallibility. In fact, her own reaction to the next revealed blooper was closer to the truth: "Children literally across continents have written and said, 'Why hasn't Marcus Flint left the school?' " she told the BBC. "He was in the fifth year when Harry started and he should have gone by book four. So I wrote back to them all and said, 'Well, Marcus Flint is so stupid he had to do another year.' Either that or I made a mistake," she joked, "but I prefer answer A."[24] The books are by no means infallible. From station problems in *Sorcerer's Stone* (Harry gets a train from Paddington—on the north bank of the River Thames—to Surrey, though Surrey is served by stations *south* of the Thames) to logistical ones in *Goblet of Fire* (echoes of Voldemort's murder victims emerge from his wand in reverse order but Harry's dad precedes his mum, though he died first), Rowling is as prone to error as anyone else.

In fact we fail to respect her identity as a *human* "sub-creator" if we demand nothing less than perfection from her creation. It is quite simply beyond any of our abilities to create perfection—that power belongs only to God. But our fallibility doesn't make our worship (including worship through sub-creation) null and void. On the contrary, it makes it all the more necessary. In fabricating the intricacy and elegance of Potterworld, Rowling (perhaps unwittingly) is worshiping her Maker. In enjoying that intricacy and elegance, we (per-haps unwittingly) are also worshiping our Maker. This isn't invali-dated just because Rowling has the boa constrictor in *Sorcerer's Stone* wink, and snakes don't have eyelids. The act of creating a "secondary world" through writing—and re-creating in our imaginations through reading—is in itself a form of worship because in doing this we are at least partially fulfilling our destiny as beings made in the im-age of God, the Creator and sustainer of all. That such a world is not perfect should not surprise us. God's image in us is, after all, marred.

It is the nature of this marring, and how Joanne Rowling ad-dresses it, which occupies the next chapter.

chapter three

THE MAN WITH TWO FACES

THE MORAL UNIVERSE
OF POTTERWORLD

~~~~

*"It was as though Wormtail had flipped over a
stone, and revealed something ugly, slimy and
blind—but worse, a hundred times worse."*[1]

All *literary* creations—whether for children
or adults—are also *moral* creations, and the
Harry Potter series is no exception. The
world of wizardry is a profoundly moral
world. Within it we find the same kind of
dilemmas, virtues, vices and characters as inhabit our own Muggle world. Making moral
decisions is every bit as messy, "fallen" and
ambiguous for Harry and his chums as it is
for us.

Understanding this is essential if we are
to avoid falling into the trap (into which
some have already tumbled) of supposing
that Joanne Rowling has opted in Potter-

world for a form of moral relativism in which there are no absolute rights and wrongs and everything is up for negotiation according to the situation (sometimes known as "situation ethics"). This is one of the criticisms leveled against her. When Harry & Co. tell fibs, act craftily and sometimes go in for wholesale deceit, their author is not advocating these things but merely being realistic both about how children behave and about the nature of moral action on the part of "fallen" human beings. In this chapter we shall see how encountering the moral universe of Potterworld enables us to reflect upon the moral nature of our own.

Morality is anything but straightforward. The BBC got it right when it called its ethical discussion program *The Moral Maze*. We may be clear that some things are *absolutely* wrong—always and everywhere inexcusably immoral—but we are rarely quite so clear about how we move from an abstract understanding of what those things are (e.g., murder) to making decisions when faced with real and irresolvable choices.

THROUGH A GLASS, DARKLY . . .

If the moral universe we live in is messy—"fallen"—then determining right and wrong is not just a case of reading from a prescribed list of dos and don'ts. Careful thought and discernment are needed. I don't say this because, as a practical theologian involved in the teaching of ethics, I have a professional interest in perpetuating the study of morality. If such "prescription" approaches to ethics really worked, I would happily hang a catalogue of dos and don'ts on the college notice board and focus on teaching other things. But discerning right and wrong is not that simple. Those who think it is are, literally, being childish—harking back to a time in their lives before they had full (legal) responsibility for their actions, when parents and teachers created a moral framework for them. As children, their job wasn't to *determine* what was right but to *do* what they were told was right (and *not* do what they were told was wrong). Things were clear-cut. Right and wrong were as distinct as the food types on their plate. There is, of course, nothing wrong with this—it is a necessary part of growing up, an essential component in learning to make our own moral choices. But if we are to function properly as adults, we have no choice but to move beyond the simplicities of childhood to recognize the complexities of adult life.

Addressing a Corinthian church filled with corruption, factionalism, greed and bitter infighting, Paul repeatedly called for *adult* thinking. He scolded Corinth's Christians for their *childish* self-righteousness, one-upmanship and know-it-all attitudes. "When I was a child," he wrote, "I spoke like a child, I thought like a child, I reasoned like a child; when I became an adult, I put an end to childish ways. For now we see in a mirror, dimly, but [when the complete comes] we will see face to face. Now I know only in part; then I will know fully."[2] Our moral imperatives, as essential as they are, offer us no more than a riddled reflection of *true* right and wrong. We see as if "through the looking glass," dim and distorted.

As a theologian who teaches ethics, part of my job is to keep polishing this mirror, always trying to improve the view. Sometimes this involves clearing away dark smudges. The Crusades, the Inquisition and the slave trade, for example, were all once seen as morally right, as were anti-Semitism and racial segregation. Worse, imagining that they knew it all, people elevated their dimly reflected moral views to the level of absolute and infallible dogma. The veteran antiapartheid campaigner Beyers Naudé, for example, was once unquestioningly sure of the moral purity and biblical credentials of his country's race laws: "The Bible supported apartheid, the Bible blessed it, and the Bible sanctioned it. And I never questioned this in any way critically," he confesses.[3] As intelligent adults, we have a responsibility to question the moral framework we inherit from society or religious tradition, rather than blindly obeying a prescribed list of dos and don'ts. And as our children grow into adolescence and adulthood—moving from simple rights and wrongs to the ever more complex moral maze of teenage years—we need to encourage them to ask difficult moral questions, too.

This is why the Potter series is such a good ethics primer. Its moral universe is closer to that of adults than infants but without losing its accessibility to younger readers. There are clear examples of right and wrong for youngsters to identify with; but there are also one or two things that will gently, and over time, begin to challenge the simplicity of their notions. In addition, there is plenty of scope for teenagers to develop their moral thinking as they get older. There are even one or two issues that hit home for adults, too.

The lack of a checklist approach to morality has led some critics to assume that Rowling's moral stance in the books is either inconsistent, indistinct or indefensible. In fact such a view is in itself naïve. What *is* true is that the Potter books are very largely free from *artificially imposed* moral lessons. The nearest Rowling gets to this are with Dumbledore's "epilogues," which on a first reading can seem a bit heavy-handed. However, if you take the time to read though the books again, these same explanations seem to flow more naturally from the great wizard's lips. The reason for this is that Potterworld's morality is carefully woven into its richly textured fabric—and as with all good literature, you tend to appreciate more of this the second time around. C. S. Lewis would have approved of this nonprescriptive, integral approach:

Let the pictures tell you their own moral. For the moral inherent in them will rise from whatever spiritual roots you have succeeded in striking during the whole course of your life. But if they don't show you any moral, don't put one in. For the moral you put in is likely to be a platitude, even a falsehood, skimmed from the surface of your consciousness. It is impertinent to offer the children that . . . The only moral that is of any value is that which arises inevitably from the whole cast of the author's mind.[4]

Like Lewis, Rowling is an intensely moral writer. And like Lewis, she is a writer whose morals are not given prescriptively but emerge naturally from the marrow of her work.

A FALLEN WORLD

The inherent morality of Potterworld is realistic, not simplistic. Between the polar extremes of absolute right (the self-sacrificial love of Harry's parents) and absolute wrong (Voldemort's evil empire) is a full spectrum of gray. Things, and particularly *people*, are rarely what they seem: Apparently bad people turn out to have redeeming features, while apparently good people turn out to have the occasional serious character flaw.

Take the two main additions to the cast list in *Azkaban*, for example: Sirius Black and Remus Lupin. Neither man is in any way straightforward. We first encounter Black in news reports about his daring and unprecedented escape from Azkaban—the Potterworld equivalent of San Francisco's infamous (and now defunct) Alcatraz Island maximum-security prison.[5] A good case is slowly built up to establish his credentials as a proper villain. We learn that, after a promising start, he defected to the Dark Lord and betrayed his best friends, James and Lily Potter, playing Judas to Voldemort's High

Priest and directly contributing to their deaths. We are told that he killed thirteen people with a single curse. We are repeatedly assured that his aim is to finish what Voldemort started and kill Harry. And in case we are tempted to think that Rowling is throwing us another red herring with all this, we are assured of his guilt when he makes two attempts to get into Gryffindor Tower. The first results in a violent assault on the Fat Lady's portrait, the second involves a knife attack on Ron Weasley's four-poster bed. Black finally abducts Ron, admitting outright that he fully intends to commit murder.

This is clearly not the behavior of an innocent man but Black *is* essentially innocent. By the end of *Azkaban*, we are sure of this, even if the wizard world is not. Appearances have, as usual with Rowling, been deceptive, and she has worked hard to make us believe them. All along we have made misguided assumptions based on partial or ambiguous evidence. Still, all is not rose petals. There are thorns too. Black may not have murdered twelve Muggles and Wormtail but he is determined to "commit the murder I was imprisoned for" by executing Wormtail anyway.⁶ He is prepared to attack both the Fat Lady and Ron, first with a knife and then, as a dog, breaking Ron's leg. If we are tempted to think that this callous and vengeful intent was bred into him by twelve years in Azkaban, it is worth noting that he survived prison by focusing on the *fact* of his innocence, not the idea of vengeance. It is also worth noting that he exhibited these tendencies while still at school, telling Snape about the Whomping Willow and thereby forcing James Potter to rescue him from certain death at the hands of a werewolf Lupin. At no point are we led to believe that Black is remorseful about this—on the contrary, he seems to think that Snape deserved such a fate. Even at the end of *Goblet of Fire*, the most the two of them can do is briefly shake hands to show that their "open hostility" is over.

Lupin, similarly, is far from morally spotless. Though he is shown in overwhelmingly positive terms at first, by the end of *Azkaban* he is just as committed as Black to lynching Wormtail. Only Harry stops them from killing in cold blood. Lupin is also guilty of "betraying Dumbledore's trust" by failing to tell him that Black is an Animagus, even after the second of Black's midnight forays into the castle and even though he believes Black to be a supporter of Voldemort. His reason—that it will mean admitting to his mentor that he "led three fellow students into becoming Animagi illegally"—seems in retrospect lame and cowardly, even to him.[7] Why he accepts Black's supposed guilt so readily, after so long and close a friendship, is also a mystery and a character flaw. Before the cock crows three times, he denies a friend who made his lupine transformations "not only bearable, but the best times of my life."[8] If anger and shock at the deaths of the Potters, and the apparent death of Wormtail, account, in part, for his initial rejection of Black, they don't account for his failure to investigate further over the next twelve years. Black's own failure to defend himself (though there is no trial) is no excuse. Would Hermione have abandoned Black? Or Harry? Undoubtedly not. We know from their bitter breakup in *Goblet of Fire*, over a far more trivial issue, that Ron might well have done so but we rightly consider that a character flaw. So it must be with Lupin. He is a positively drawn character but one with definite feet of clay.

The opposite—a negatively drawn character with redeeming qualities—is seen in the archetype of moral ambiguity in Potterworld: Professor Severus Snape. It is always tempting to pigeonhole Snape one way or the other. For most of *Sorcerer's Stone*, and for much of *Chamber of Secrets*, he is cast in the role of chief bad guy. He is our prime suspect when it comes to acquiring the Stone for Voldemort and petrifying students as Slytherin's Heir. When he is shown to have been innocent of these accusations, we are then tempted to cast him in the role of good guy but here he confounds us again. His successful attempts to save Harry from Quirrell's curse in the Gryffindor-Slytherin Quidditch match and his vain attempts to save Quirrell from Voldemort must be set against his clear bias in favor of Slytherin students, his unfair decision-making as a teacher and his real *hatred* of Harry. His willingness to prepare Lupin's Wolfsbane Potion in *Azkaban* is ruined by the vindictiveness that makes him willing to hand Black over to the Dementors for summary execution, subject Lupin to the same fate (though he has committed no crime), and let a guilty man walk (or scurry off) free rather than listen to the evidence and admit he might have been wrong. Snape's ambiguity is so complete that, for most of *Goblet of Fire*, we can't entirely shake off the suspicion that he really *is* Voldemort's "faithful servant at Hogwarts." Only at the end does it become clear that, having once been a Death Eater, he has truly burned his bridges and chosen to side *with* Dumbledore (and therefore Harry) *against* Voldemort.

If we are honest, most of us know only too well how compromised and corrupt we are. We identify fairly readily with Paul's confession to the Romans, "I do not do the good I want, but the evil I do not want is what I do."[9] Most of us gradually learn to face and deal with our inadequacies. We start in infancy, in our first years at school, when we learn that we may not be the cleverest, or prettiest, or most popular, or most musically or sportingly gifted child in class. If we receive enough encouragement and affirmation from those around us, we will be able to put these weaknesses and limitations into perspective by setting them alongside our newly discovered strengths and skills but we delude ourselves if we imagine, even for a moment, that we or others can be either *all* good or *all* bad. "If we say that we have no sin, we deceive ourselves," warned John.[10] We are all "fallen" and sinful beings but at the same time we have been created in the image of a perfect God whose Spirit is continually at work in us. We are neither angel nor beast. Our moral universe is more complicated than that.

It is to Rowling's credit that she presents this honestly and understandably through the creation of characters with real moral gray areas. It is to her credit, also, that she has sketched amidst these shades of gray some highlights and lowlights in starker tones of black and white, so that a pattern begins to emerge. Younger readers will see *only* these highlights and lowlights—they will read, but not fully understand, about the gray. They will *like* Black and Lupin (ignoring their murderous designs) and *dislike* Snape (though they won't put him in the same class as Voldemort). Slightly older readers, such as twelve- or fifteen-year-olds, will see *both* the highlights and lowlights *and* the gray. Hopefully, they will see in the pattern of starker black and white a key to help them discern various different shades amid the gray. They will find it increasingly hard just to dismiss the serious character flaws of Lupin and Black, or to fit Snape into straightforward good/bad stereotypes. Instead, they will have begun to acquire a real sense of moral discernment.

AWAKENINGS

As the series continues, it is likely that Rowling will find it harder to blend together the morally simple and complex. In part this is because as Harry gets older, the moral choices presented to him, and the moral choices he makes, will (if he remains true to life) undoubtedly become tougher. At seventeen, in his final year at Hogwarts, Harry will surely have a much better understanding of truth and deceit than he does at eleven (his first year). With such an understanding inevitably comes more moral responsibility, taking Harry farther away from the structured and simple universe he, Ron and Hermione share in their pre-adolescence. The more skilled and adept he becomes at interpreting shades of gray, and making his moral decisions accordingly, the less young readers will understand the reasons for his choosing to act as he does. His actual choices may be clear enough but his motivation—and therefore his character—will become increasingly complex and difficult to comprehend. It will take great literary skill for Rowling to make his character and conscience at one and the same time credible for older readers and understandable for younger ones.

Harry's *moral* awakening through the series has received considerably less attention in the media than his hormonal awakening but it is in many ways more prevalent and important. At the start of *Sorcerer's Stone*, for example, he and his friends are generally obedient to rules. Harry stays where he is put in the Cupboard under the Stairs and largely does what the Dursleys tell him to do, even though their treatment of him is extremely unfair and they would—outside a fairy tale—be liable for criminal prosecution. He generally does what he is told at Hogwarts, too, and when he *does* break rules, he sees his disobedience as wrongdoing. The same can be said for Ron and, in particular, Hermione. In contrast to the views of some critics—who see in Potterworld an encouragement to flagrant disobedience and rule breaking—the three friends begin as consummate rule followers. What is more, like most children, they change very slowly, remaining predominantly rule followers for most of the first four books.

When Dumbledore notes that Harry, like Salazar Slytherin, has "a certain disregard for rules,"[11] therefore, we should not get the wrong idea. Harry does indeed break rules but his motivation is rarely expediency or selfishness (and when it is, Rowling generally portrays the results as being mixed, at best). Instead, he finds that obedience to the rules can clash directly with obedience to a higher moral principle: loyalty to one's friends, for example, or saving the world. It is a major break with the clear-cut, rule-following infant mind-set of all three friends when Hermione tells a "downright lie" to Professor McGonagall in order to get Ron and Harry off the hook after their run-in with an angry troll. The two boys have disobeyed instructions (intended to keep them out of harm's way) not from a sense of deliberate mischief but for the more noble purpose of alerting Hermione to the troll threat. Perhaps they would have been better to have alerted a member of the staff—in the circumstances, that would have been the *right* thing to do; but it would have entailed admitting that Hermione had been absent all afternoon because Ron had been mean to her once too often, and (like Lupin) they didn't yet have the moral courage for that. Hermione, in turn, is motivated by loyalty and friendship above pure obedience when she tells McGonagall that Ron and Harry had come looking for her because she had decided to fight the troll single-handed:

> *Harry was speechless. Hermione was the last person to do anything against the rules, and here she was, pretending she had, to get them out of trouble. It was as if Snape had started handing out sweets.*[12]

On the face if it, this involves moving *down* a rung on the moral ladder, from obedience to disobedience, from honesty to dishonesty. However, appearances are deceptive. Harry and his friends are *not* learning to be disobedient or dishonest: Most children learn these "skills" as toddlers or (at the latest) infants, and there is no reason to suppose that even Hermione was an exception on that score. The friends are, instead, learning that moral principles can sometimes conflict with one another. In this instance, obedience to the rules conflicts with concern for a friend. Hermione doesn't tell a lie to get herself out of trouble—the lie gets her *into* trouble. She takes the blame for something she hasn't done in order to protect Harry and Ron, just as they broke the rules to protect her. We could argue that their behavior was "both very brave and very stupid"[13]—Rowling would agree. But if their actions are not the *best* they could have come up with, they still represent a shift *up* the moral ladder, from the blind obedience proper to infancy to a more mature recognition that moral imperatives (obedience and friendship, for example) can sometimes compete with one another. They have begun to move from a simple commitment to the rules to a commitment to those moral principles that *underlie* the rules.

In Corrie ten Boom's book *The Hiding Place*, she recalls how, living in Nazi-occupied Holland during World War II, her family had been part of the "underground railway," hiding Jewish families from the Germans and ferrying them to safety. On one occasion her brothers returned home in a dash, hotly pursued by pro-Nazi policemen. There was no time to conceal them in one of their special hiding places, so they hid them under the kitchen table, obscured from sight by nothing more than a tablecloth. When the officer in charge questioned the other family members, they replied that the "unknown" men had run into the house (they couldn't deny this) and left immediately by the back door. However, when asked the same question, Corrie ten Boom's infant niece told the truth. Corrie's sister had brought up her children *never* to lie, so the young girl calmly replied that the men were hidden just a few feet away, beneath the table. Corrie's heart missed a beat—all the officer had to do was lift the cloth to confirm what she had said. Fortunately, he did nothing. Perhaps he didn't want to look foolish in front of his men by checking and finding the space empty. For whatever reason, he instead ordered his men to leave. It was a narrow escape.

Most of us, I think, can understand the response of Corrie's niece. Brought up to be obedient and honest, hers was a typical infant response. It is not, of course, what *I* would have done, and it was not what the rest of the family did. They realized that protecting your loved ones can be more important than telling the absolute truth when you can't do both. This is the same moral lesson that Hermione learns. We could argue that *her* lie was not really necessary, and I think we would be right but that doesn't alter the fact that, for her, it is a watershed. Her moral universe starts to change from that of an infant to that of an adult.

This, I think, rather than an irresponsible desire to encourage children to break the rules, is why Rowling presents this episode in a positive light. When, fifteen pages earlier, Harry and Ron disobey the curfew and wander the castle en route to a supposed midnight duel with Malfoy, she is far more negative and depicts them as breaking rules for no good reason. Their foolish pride nearly gets them into serious trouble. Hermione accompanies them under protest: In her attempts to dissuade them (on the grounds that it is against the rules and could lead to house points being taken off Gryffindor—a typical infant response), she accidentally locks herself out of Gryffindor Tower. Though the trip introduces them all to Fluffy, Hagrid's many-headed monster dog, and the whereabouts of the trapdoor, it is still portrayed as a silly mistake. As Hermione notes, "We could all have been killed—or worse, expelled."[14] It drives a wedge between Harry and Ron, on the one hand, and Hermione and Neville (who goes with them because he, too, is locked out of Gryffindor Tower) on the other. By contrast, Harry and Ron's effort to warn Hermione about the troll is painted in more positive colors. And rather than pushing the three of them farther apart, it cements their friendship.

In the dénouement of *Sorcerer's Stone*, Harry, Ron and Hermione find themselves on the horns of a moral dilemma when they discover that Voldemort's servant knows how to get past all of the magical protections around the Stone. They opt to take their information to Dumbledore, as they *should* have done with the troll, but he is absent and McGonagall is not willing to believe that three eleven-year-olds have detected a weakness in the Stone's security that the entire school staff has not. They face a tough choice: to do as they are told and ignore the threat to the Stone, or to break the rules and take on the trapdoor's terrors themselves. It is a choice between accepting the moral responsibility (and risk) that goes with their knowledge or washing their hands of the problem. The decision to go ahead represents not irresponsible rule breaking but a triumph of adult moral reasoning over infant moral reflex.

Of course, development doesn't happen overnight, and when all three friends attack the unhinged Snape in *Azkaban*, they find it hard to come to terms with their actions:

> *"We attacked a teacher . . . we attacked a teacher . . ."* Hermione whimpered, *staring at the lifeless Snape with frightened eyes. "Oh, we're going to be in so much trouble——"*[15]

These are not the words of a true rebel. Even though they have done the morally *right* thing—saving the lives of two innocent men and trying to ensure that a guilty one is tried—Hermione and the others still having considerable trouble adjusting to the fact that the *right* thing may not always be the obedient thing. Sometimes obedience and goodness clash.

By *Goblet of Fire*, of course, they are all becoming more adept at discerning right and wrong and choosing the appropriate action. Harry, for example, has always known that his Uncle Vernon's treatment of him is unjust but he has always gone along with his tyrannical behavior and regulations before. Now, at fourteen—having bravely faced up to genuine evil and defeated it—he "wasn't going to stand for" his uncle's shameless bullying tactics any more. "Gone were the days when he had been forced to take every single one of the Dursleys' stupid rules."[16] Here at last, perhaps, Rowling encourages teenage rebellion—except that the Dursleys' behavior toward Harry is consistently *abusive*, and Harry's way of coping with it isn't outright disobedience but an attempt to use their own prejudices and pretensions against them. He is demonstrating a mature ability to recognize wrong and respond to it in a firm, measured way.

TOTAL CONTROL

The importance of developing this kind of responsible moral independence, rather than mere rule-following, is examined most fully in *Goblet of Fire*. Discussion centers on the complex moral issues of free will, influence and determinism, which Rowling explores by looking at the fate of the former Death Eaters and the Imperius curse.

After Voldemort's fall from power, most of those who had supported him through his reign of terror, either as proper Death Eaters or as functionaries, suddenly found themselves without his brutal protection. Facing the prospect of public recriminations and Nuremberg-style tribunals, many switched allegiance to the winning side. Some, like Bagman, claimed they had been duped, acting in innocence and ignorance. Some, like Karkaroff, admitted their guilt but cut deals with the avenging angel of the prosecution, Magical Law Enforcement boss Crouch the Elder. In this way they secured their freedom in exchange for the names of former co-conspirators. But many, like the weak-willed Avery, claimed that they had never actually been a supporter of Voldemort and had instead been *forced* to act on his behalf as the result of an Imperius curse.

The Imperius curse gave Voldemort and his henchmen the ability, in Black's words, to "control people so that they do terrible things without being able to stop themselves."[17] A very effective form of hypnosis, the bogus Moody calls it "total control."

> *"Years back, there were a lot of witches and wizards being controlled by the Imperius curse," said Moody, and Harry knew he was talking about the days in which Voldemort had been all-powerful. "Some job for the Ministry, trying to sort out who was being forced to act, and who was acting out of their own free will."*[18]

But in fact the Imperius curse does *not* offer a dark magician *total control*. As Moody himself admits—speaking, we later realize, from the personal experience of having eventually resisted his father's Imperius curse—it can be fought. "It takes," he adds, "real strength of character, and not everyone's got it."[19] We must assume that *everyone* subjected to the curse hears two voices, like Harry: the one that accompanies the floating, dreaming sensation and orders them to do something, and the one that comes from the back of their head and tells them to resist. This is, effectively, the voice of conscience; and Rowling clearly sees an advantage for those who learn to help it assert itself over the near-overwhelming pressure to go with the flow.

"The gate is wide and the road is easy that leads to destruction," warned Jesus, "and there are many who take it. For the gate is narrow and the road is hard that leads to life, and there are few who find it."[20] When Voldemort tells Harry that "obedience is a virtue I need to teach you before you die,"[21] we recognize this type of "obedience" as the "easy road" that leads to destruction; in such circumstances, *dis*obedience is the *right* course of action—the "hard road" that leads to life. But it is Harry's growing sense of moral independence—forged from experience in more trivial matters, and the occasional mistake— that enables him to choose the narrow gate over the wide one when it matters. If all he had been taught at Hogwarts—and all Rowling had taught in Potterworld—was a prescriptive morality, rather than a developing moral awareness and conscience, Harry would never have had sufficient moral fiber to resist the Imperius curse or stand up to the risen Lord Voldemort.

The complex interaction between natural moral behavior on one hand and personal decision and action on the other are integral to Rowling's idea of morality. Both are shown as real and powerful factors in shaping who the characters become; but neither is seen as ultimately determinative. Just as the evil Imperius curse can be fought, so elements of our personalities can be shaped by the different moral choices we make. Harry is nagged by self-doubt through most of *Chamber of Secrets*, because in *Sorcerer's Stone* the Sorting Hat briefly considered putting him in Slytherin, causing him to wonder whether his inner nature was nearer the ethos of Slytherin than Gryffindor. When "enemies of the Heir" are petrified, and Harry is found to be a Parselmouth, he begins to wonder if perhaps he *is* Slytherin's Heir— if he *should* be in Slytherin house or inevitably *will* turn out to be a dark wizard. Even Slytherin's true Heir, Voldemort, wonders about Harry:

> "There are strange likenesses between us, Harry Potter: Even you must have noticed. Both half-bloods, orphans, raised by Muggles. Probably the only two Parselmouths to come to Hogwarts since the great Slytherin himself. We even look something alike."[22]

When Harry asks, Dumbledore admits that there are indeed qualities in him that Salazar Slytherin looked for in his handpicked students, just as there are similarities with Voldemort and his former self, Tom Riddle. (In *Goblet of Fire* we are reminded that the Phoenix feather in Harry's wand is the twin of that in Voldemort's.) Thus is the role of nature in shaping human character acknowledged. There are elements in Harry's nature that could have helped him to go bad. But at the same time, there are also qualities in him that Godric Gryffindor admired—elements in his nature that help him to be good. Harry could have gone either way, and still can. The potential for evil is there. But the difference, as Harry himself admits, is that he "asked not to go in Slytherin"—"Which," Dumbledore patiently explains, "makes you very *different* from Tom Riddle. It is our choices, Harry, that show what we truly are, far more than our abilities."[23] Thus is one of the major themes of ethics—the relationship between free will and determinism—raised. It is no mean feat.

"STARK, GRIM AND COLOSSALLY REAL"

Rowling does not, of course, pull many punches in her depiction of evil. Even adult readers—perhaps *especially* adult readers—experience a sharp intake of breath at the murders in *Goblet of Fire*. The killing of Cedric Diggory, in particular, is made all the more dreadful because of the callous and almost casual way in which it is done: "*Kill the spare.*"[24] There are no grisly details, of course—describing troll bogies is one thing, and very appealing to children but the anatomy of a murder is something utterly different; and Rowling achieves her effect without having to resort to the kind of gore that would make the work inaccessible to younger readers. Nevertheless, she manages to get across the fact that evil is, in the words of Martin Luther King, "stark, grim and colossally real."[25] This has, predictably, led to concern and censure but Rowling defends the darkening tone of her work; "I am writing about someone, Voldemort, who is evil. And rather than make him a pantomime villain, the only way of showing how evil it is to take a life is to kill someone the reader cares about."[26]

This may be an overstatement—we never *really* care about Diggory, who appears in *Goblet of Fire* as a straw man, there to be killed in a blast of green light. Nevertheless, Rowling does try not to make pantomime villains or pantomime villainies. Potterworld is awash with real evil, in multiple shades and guises.

Take the issue of racism, for example, which surfaces in the form of wizards' attitudes to half-giants like Hagrid and, of course, to Muggles like us. In both cases, it is the pureblood Draco Malfoy who makes us aware of the prejudice. Hagrid, he observes through the window of Madam Malkin's robe shop, is, "A sort of savage—lives in a hut in the school grounds and every now and then he gets drunk, tries to do magic and ends up setting fire to his bed."[27] We are reminded of the kind of comments made about Africans during the colonial era or about African Americans during slavery and Segregation, though we have to wait for *Goblet of Fire* to find out how widespread this kind of sentiment is throughout the wizard world. Malfoy's view of Muggles is no better. Asking Harry if his dead parents were "*our* kind," he remarks:

> "*I really don't think they should let the other sort in, do you? They're just not the same, they've never been brought up to know our ways. Some of them have never even heard of Hogwarts until they get the letter, imagine. I think they should keep it in the old wizarding families.*"[28]

Rowling clearly sets herself against this kind of thinking by introducing it through a character we have already learned to dislike. And we see its folly even more because Harry himself, though a wizarding legend, has never heard of Hogwarts until he gets his letter.

Over time, however, the issue becomes slightly more complicated. On the one hand, the fallacy of anti-Mugglism is shown for what it is through the revelation that neither Harry nor Voldemort are pureblood. Harry's maternal grandparents, like Aunt Petunia, were Muggles, as was Voldemort's father. And with Lord Voldemort, the irony deepens: It is *he* who opens the Chamber of Secrets as the last remaining true Heir and descendant of Hogwarts' founder Salazar Slytherin. Yet Slytherin himself, as Professor Binns explains, wasn't just a pureblood but also a firm anti-Mugglist:

> *"Slytherin wanted to be more* selective *about the students admitted to Hogwarts. He believed that magical learning should be kept within all-magic families. He disliked taking students of Muggle parentage, believing them to be untrustworthy."*[29]

On the other hand, the extent of anti-Mugglism is shown up by the fact that it isn't merely the Malfoys and other negatively drawn characters who exhibit disdain for so-called Mudbloods. One or two of the more positively drawn characters do so as well. It is never entirely clear, for example, whether Severus Snape is a "Muggle-lover" or not but Minister of Magic Cornelius Fudge emerges in *Goblet of Fire* as a character who is not only as blustering and bumbling as his name suggests but avaricious and bigoted. As Professor Dumbledore pointedly remarks, "You place too much importance, and you always have, on the so-called purity of blood! You fail to recognize that it matters not what someone is born but what they grow to be!"[30]

If Rowling's views about racism are generally fairly clear, however—at times so clear as to be almost propagandist—the issue of slavery is less explicitly handled. It is no doubt safe to assume that she herself is as antislavery in her opinions as most of her readers. Nevertheless, the issue appears more complicated in her books than one might expect. When Hermione learns that house-elves are being "employed" at Hogwarts, she begins a campaign that garners virtually no support. Harry and Ron are the only real members of SPEW, her Society for the Protection of Elfish Welfare, and they join only because, as Hermione's best friends, they have no real choice. Even the house-elves themselves don't want what she wants to secure for them: pay, pensions, sick leave and holidays. Dobby is the *only* house-elf with any interest in freedom, perhaps because he used to belong to the Malfoys. But even he appears to have problems grasping some of the fundamentals:

> *"Professor Dumbledore offered Dobby ten Galleons a week, and weekends off,"* said Dobby, suddenly giving a little shiver, as though the prospect of so much leisure and riches was frightening, *"but Dobby beat him down, miss . . . Dobby likes freedom, miss, but he isn't wanting too much, miss, he likes work better."*[31]

This is undoubtedly funny but it is not yet clear how the issue will develop. One possibility is that, given Rowling's clear antiracism, her portrayal of the house-elves contains a message about not assuming that others will share her own highly moral views. Alternatively, she may be opening up a line of thinking that has yet to develop. We can only wait and see.

What is clear from the house-elf question is the light it sheds on the issue of bullying. "If you want to know what a man's like," Black advises Ron, "take a good look at how he treats his inferiors, not his equals."[32] When Crouch sacks Winky—supposedly for disobeying him and leaving his tent but actually for allowing his son to leave the tent and for having talked him into letting his son go to the Quidditch World Cup in the first place—he reveals his true colors. The failure to control his son is *his*, not his elf's—a failure that stretches back not merely to his escape from Azkaban but right back to childhood. Crouch has seemingly never shown his son the love and tenderness he deserves as a human being, having instead single-mindedly "dedicated his whole life to becoming Minister for Magic."[33] The sacking of Winky mirrors the cruelty he exhibits at his son's trial (which he improperly presides over)—not only is there no sign of compassion, but more important, there is no recognition of his own role and responsibility. He attempts, like Pontius Pilate, to wash his hands of the whole affair, blaming his son or Winky rather than admitting his own guilt; and like Pontius Pilate, his attempts are far from convincing.

Rowling makes strong connections between the kind of bullying that goes on among children—Dudley's bullying of Harry, for example—and the kind that goes on among adults. It can be tempting to imagine that bullying is merely a childhood problem, but Rowling makes it clear that what begins in childhood will, if not tackled, continue into adulthood. Draco Malfoy is a bully at school and looks set to follow in his father Lucius' footsteps by becoming a bully as an adult. Lucius may have more refined tactics than his son but he is still a bully, maltreating Dobby and pressuring fellow Hogwarts governors into suspending Dumbledore in *Chamber of Secrets*. "The other eleven governors contacted me today," Dumbledore explains when the suspension is lifted. "Several of them seemed to think that you had threatened to curse their families if they didn't agree to suspend me in the first place."[34]

TWO WRONGS

Of course, not all ways of dealing with bullying, and with evil, are equally valid. McGonagall makes it very clear that the bogus Moody's method of punishing Malfoy—turning him into a ferret and bouncing him on the stone floor—is unacceptable. (We realize later that Moody is in fact taking revenge on Malfoy for belonging to a family that deserted Voldemort after his fall.) This is part of an ongoing thread throughout the Potter series. Just as Rowling believes that evil is real, so she is convinced that not every way of combating it is morally justified.

This view arises in the very first chapter of *Sorcerer's Stone*. When McGonagall notes that Dumbledore is the only wizard Voldemort has ever been frightened of, Dumbledore replies that "Voldemort had powers I will never have." McGonagall counters: "Only because you're too—well—*noble* to use them."[35] This is true; but Dumbledore's "nobility" is at heart very practical. He eschews the manipulative and ruthless tactics of Voldemort and others, not because of an abstract concept of gentlemanly behavior but because he knows that *ends* and *means* are fused together. As Martin Luther King said, "Ultimately, you can't reach good ends through evil means, because the means represent the seed and the end represents the tree."[36]

It is an ethos deeply embodied in Harry himself, who consistently refuses to repay like for like (even on a trivial level with Malfoy). When, in *Azkaban*, he has a chance to kill Black in vengeance, as he sees it, for the death of his parents, he cannot go through with it.[37] He is not willing to use summary justice and take a life for a life. And when Lupin and Black join forces to murder the *real* traitor, Wormtail, he stops them by stepping between them and their intended victim. This is not mere sentimentality or bleeding-heart liberalism: it is coolheaded reasoning. As he explains to Wormtail, "I'm not doing this for you. I'm doing it because I don't reckon my dad would've wanted his best friends to become killers—just for you."[38]

The opposite approach is taken by Crouch the Elder, a firm believer in the old adage about fighting fire with fire. As Black explains:

> *"Crouch's principles might've been good in the beginning—I wouldn't know. He rose quickly through the Ministry, and he started ordering very harsh measures against Voldemort's supporters. The Aurors were given*

new powers—powers to kill rather than capture, for instance. And I wasn't the only one who was handed straight to the Dementors without trial. Crouch fought violence with violence, and authorized the use of the Unforgivable Curses against suspects. I would say he became as ruthless and cruel as many on the Dark side."[39]

For Crouch and others this kind of behavior proves fatal. Crouch's cruelty surfaces in his relations with his son, to whom he shows no love. Perhaps this lack of affection from someone who supposedly represents *goodness* is one of the things that pushes the son into the clutches of Voldemort (to whom he is "closer than a son").

In the end, Crouch reaps the whirlwind of his actions. He sacrifices his son on the altar of his ambition only to have the top job snatched away at the last minute by his son's criminal behavior. ("Should have spent a bit more time at home with his family, shouldn't he? Ought to have left the office early once in a while . . . got to know his own son.")[40] He prejudices the jury's verdict in his son's trial (with the result that no one is sure whether he is guilty or not) but has to smuggle him out of Azkaban later to appease his dying wife. He covers up this crime by permanently damaging the memory of Bertha Jorkins, only to have her cause more trouble by vanishing on holiday (where she is murdered and her suppressed memory acquired by Voldemort). He uses the Imperius curse to control his son, then finds it used on himself when Voldemort returns. Finally, he pays for his renunciation of his son (he hands down the sentence with the words, "I have no son") when Crouch the Younger joins Lord Voldemort as one who has "had the pleasure . . . the very great pleasure . . . of killing our fathers."[41]

Fudge, however—the man who becomes Minister of Magic in place of Crouch—is not a vast improvement. His reliance on the loathsome Dementors to keep dark wizards in check is reminiscent of the Black Dwarfs' reliance on Ogres, Hags and the White Witch's power in the fight against the wicked tyrant Miraz in Lewis's *Prince Caspian*. Under the control of the Dementors, Azkaban offers no possibility of reform for prisoners—all their hope and positive feelings are sucked out. The Dementors don't so much guard their charges as *feed on* them. Sirius Black survives a dozen years because he obsesses on the cold hard *fact* of his innocence; most prisoners, innocent or guilty, go insane. This is not a just or humane form of punishment; but Fudge defends it, as he defends a Dementor's disposal of Crouch the Younger without due legal process. "Kiss" first, ask questions later. Dumbledore is not merely speaking for himself when he warns Fudge to remove Azkaban from the control of the Dementors:

> *"You have put Lord Voldemort's most dangerous supporters in the care of creatures who will join him the instant he asks them!" said Dumbledore. "They will not remain loyal to you, Fudge! Voldemort can offer them much more scope for their powers and their pleasures than you can!"*[42]

Perhaps even more worryingly, however, Fudge's willingness to use nefarious means to achieve glorious ends is coupled with a stubborn refusal to see the dangers around him, especially after the return of Voldemort. Not only does he reject all of Dumbledore's demands for action, he even rejects Dumbledore's assertion that Voldemort has risen again. He remains absolutely determined not to see the awful truth if at all possible. The seriousness of the situation calls for a "parting of the ways" between the two men, and there are echoes of Martin Luther King's advice that "to ignore evil is to become an accomplice to it"[43] in Dumbledore's warning to Fudge: "Fail to act—and history will remember you as the man who stepped aside, and allowed Voldemort a second chance to destroy the world we have tried to rebuild!"[44]

"ALL FOR ONE AND ONE FOR ALL!"

The moral universe of Potterworld is one in which there is real evil and real good. The evil must be fought, the good must be embraced. But, of course, this is as true within characters as it is between them. "There is some good in the worst of us and some evil in the best of us," as King put it. This idea stands at the heart of the Potter saga, in its characters and stories. From it arises the moral lesson that, consciously or not, Rowling gives above all others: that none of us is perfect, and we all need each other to keep us on the straight and narrow.

It is a lesson that is drawn negatively in the fractured relationship between Moony, Wormtail, Padfoot and Prongs in *Azkaban*, for example, and more positively in the mutually dependent relationship between Harry, Ron and Hermione that runs continuously throughout the entire series. The differences, rooted deep in the characters, are instructive. The tendency of the school quartet of Moony Lupin, Wormtail Pettigrew, Padfoot Black and Prongs Potter simply to laugh off the "near misses" of their adolescent antics—the midnight roams with the werewolf Moony that eventually result in the creation of the mischievous Marauder's Map—rather than to learn from these mistakes and keep each other in check, surely contributes to the gradual distancing of their friendship. Over time, it drifts to a point where Padfoot and Moony both suspect each other of passing information to Voldemort, and neither of them realizes that the true culprit is Wormtail . . . or why. Aware of not being "in their league, talent-wise"[45] but unaware of just how vital the mutual friendship and support of all *four* of them is to the proper use of those talents (of whatever league), Wormtail is easy pickings for Voldemort. The chain of friendship, only as strong as its weakest link, breaks because the other three, for whatever reasons, fail to give Wormtail the support he needs to resist the "weapons you can't imagine" that

Voldemort unleashes on him. The results, for all four, are catastrophic. They are brought down by Voldemort and dark magic because they do not fight it together in mutual support.

By contrast, when Ron and Hermione fall out over Crookshanks the cat in *Azkaban*, and again over the Yule Ball in *Goblet of Fire*, they have Harry to keep them on the straight and narrow and to bring them back to a point of reconciliation. And when Ron and Harry fall out over the Triwizard championship in *Goblet of Fire*, Hermione similarly remains friend to both and helps them overcome their differences. Harry and Ron are there to keep Hermione's house-elf obsession in check; Harry and Hermione are there to keep Ron's blistering temper under control; and Ron and Hermione are there to keep Harry's spirits up, to help him find answers to the challenges he faces, and to deal with the emotional consequences of both his summers with the Dursleys and his confrontations with Voldemort. Each acts as a brake on the others' vices, and as a spur to their virtues. They stand or fall together.

FINALLY . . .

We have seen how, far from being amoral or immoral, as some have supposed, Potterworld is a highly moral place. While not overtly Christian, the values it espouses resonate at critical points with Christian morality: loyalty, fidelity, honesty (in the deepest sense), courage, trust and, above all, love are prominent virtues worked out in the lives of our heroes, while the reality of evil and wrongdoing are clearly brought out and condemned. In book after book, evil fails as goodness triumphs. The Christian belief in the vindication of the Good finds itself reflected, albeit in nonreligious terms. Moreover, the wisdom and compassion of Albus Dumbledore echo the kind of wisdom we find in the book of Proverbs, with its combination of ethical realism and virtuous behavior.

True, the reader will search in vain for an explicitly religious ethic, since it is simply not there. Still less is there anything resembling a Christ-centered morality. For those who are willing only to accept explicitly Christian teaching, this will be a disappointment. But for myself, I am glad that Rowling expounds both the complex realism of moral decision-making and the existence of fundamental virtues while at the same time recognizing the struggle between good and evil. Compared to the stream of amoral trash that pervades our film and television screens (I speak as one who likes both of these media), the Harry Potter books are to be lauded as an unrivaled way into ethical reasoning for children who would otherwise be exposed to the cancerous relativism of our age.

chapter four

THE DEATH EATERS

THE THEOLOGY
OF POTTERWORLD

*"So. Your mother died to save you. Yes, that's a
powerful counter-charm. I can see now—there is
nothing special about you, after all."*[1]

It may seem strange to include in this book a
chapter on the *theology* of Potterworld—after all, God hardly gets a passing reference
anywhere in the books except as a swear
word on the lips of Draco Malfoy. On the
face of it there would seem to *be* no theology
of Potterworld. But there is in fact a considerable amount of traditional Christian theology implicitly reflected in the pages of
Potterworld. It may not be as obvious as the
theology to be found in Lewis's Narnia
books, and it is certainly nothing like as self-
conscious but it is there nonetheless. It
emerges in two distinct forms: in the superfi-

cial vestiges of Christianity that are still present in both the Muggle and the magical cultures of Potterworld (as they are still present in our own culture); and also in the richer themes that are more characteristic of Christian theology (if not always exclusive to it) which permeate the Potter books at a much deeper level. We shall look at each in turn.

OH COME, ALL YE FATEFUL . . .

Christianity has had a profound and lasting impact on British culture. For almost 1,500 years, it has been the dominant national religion. And according to a national survey published by Christian Research for the year 2000, it still is: Sixty-five percent of the English population considers itself Christian (though only 8 percent actually goes to church on any given Sunday morning). The figures are likely to be higher, if anything, for Scotland, Wales and Northern Ireland. What is more, the culture in this country remains saturated with significant amounts of Christian practice and belief. Christmas and Easter, for example, are still the main national festivities, and the public celebration of them continues to presuppose a modest knowledge of Christian doctrine. A national poster campaign launched last Christmas to advertise a well-known brand of rum contained the caption: "No room at the inn? Don't go to bed!" The campaign relied on the fact that most people seeing it would know enough of the nativity story to make the connection with Mary and Joseph and get the joke.

Such cultural vestiges of Christianity are found in Potterworld, too. The prime feast of the Hogwarts school year is Halloween, of course, but school terms are arranged around the traditional Christian holidays of Christmas and Easter; and Harry and his friends still give and receive Christmas presents. And although Rowling chooses to name the Yule Ball in *Goblet of Fire* after the ancient twelve-day pagan festival that coincided with (and was taken over by) Christmas, there are nevertheless most of the trappings of what we would call a "traditional Christmas celebration"—except, of course, any acknowledgment whatsoever of Jesus Christ.

It is tempting, therefore, for us as Christians to berate J. K. Rowling for having left the Christ out of Christmas. But the sad fact is that for perhaps the majority of the population what she has left *in* is wholly representative of what Christmas is and means. Only a few will have noticed the absence of Jesus. The day follows a predictable and traditional format, starting with presents and continuing with a full turkey-and-trimmings lunch, complete with crackers and Christmas pudding. To her credit, Rowling makes *giving* presents as much of an issue as *receiving* them, and we can only hope that this continues as Harry matures, enabling younger readers gradually to appreciate the wisdom of Jesus' assurance that "it is more blessed to give than to receive."[2] Equally creditable is her insistence that Christmas is a family occasion. Harry may be pleased to be staying at Hogwarts for the holidays, away from his uncle and aunt but it gives him the chance to spend the time with what is to all intents and purposes his *real* family: Dumbledore, Hagrid, the Weasleys and Hermione. As George tells his brother Percy, "You're not sitting with the Prefects today . . . Christmas is a time for family."[3]

Rowling does, however, present us with a neat and highly useful, if perhaps unwitting, model of how both characters in Potterworld and our society as a whole respond to Christmas and the Christian faith in general:

> *The usual twelve Christmas trees in the Great Hall were bedecked with everything from luminous holly berries to real, hooting, golden owls, and the suits of armor had all been bewitched to sing carols whenever anyone*

passed them. It was quite something to hear, "Oh Come, All Ye Faithful"
sung by an empty helmet that only knew half the words. Several times,
Filch the caretaker had to extract Peeves from inside the armor, where he
had taken to hiding, filling in the gaps in the songs with lyrics of his own
invention, all of which were very rude.[4]

Suits of armor sing Christmas carols but know only half the words—
this is both literally and metaphorically representative of a large number of people for whom carols are as important a part of the Christmas
season as mulled wine, mince pies and even midnight mass. Not only
do they not know half the words, they also don't understand more
than half the meaning. Perhaps even Rowling herself belongs in this
category. If so, we can hardly blame her—any more than we can
blame the British public as a whole—for "filling in the gaps" in her
knowledge of the Christmas story with "lyrics of her own invention."

In fact, most of the references to Christmas that occur in the
Potter series appear to be little more than the half-invented lyrics of
previous generations. For example, Christmas Day itself was in the
Middle Ages a tiny feast compared with Twelfth Night, celebrated on
January 6, which marked the end of the Christmas period and was an
occasion of real merrymaking. Turkey only replaced goose or beef in
the Christmas meal in the late 1500s, and Christmas pudding wasn't
introduced until about 1670. Mistletoe, holly and other evergreen
plants and trees are ancient hangovers from the pagan Yule festival,
where they were considered refuges for tree spirits once deciduous
trees had lost their leaves but they really came into their own once
Christmas trees became widespread in the Victorian era, thanks (so it
is said) to Prince Albert.

In many ways, what we think of as Christmas is a largely
Victorian invention, owing its so-called "traditional" form almost entirely to one man—Charles Dickens. The Victorians revived the

singing of carols (originally medieval festival dance tunes) and wrote most of the ones we are now familiar with; they imported the French idea of tying up bundles of sweets for children and turned it into the Christmas cracker; they stressed the importance of family celebrations and of generosity and present-giving; they created the mystique of snow and sentimentality; and they manufactured and sent the first Christmas card. In fact besides the Queen's Speech, about the only "essential ingredient" of a modern British Christmas that we do not owe to the Victorians is Santa Claus—an American creation fusing together the English idea of Father Christmas (a red-robed personification of Christmas), the European idea of Saint Nicholas and the ancient Scandinavian legend of a magician who rewarded good children with presents.

Ironically, it is these fairly recent embellishments—not the celebration of Jesus' birth, which dates back at least to the early fourth century—that have survived the steady decline of Christian influence on society. These late Christmas rituals represent most of the lyrics that people *can* remember. It is when it comes to the true *meaning* of Christmas, the story of the incarnation, that gaps begin to appear in people's memories—gaps that are then filled with lyrics of our own invention. Christmas basically becomes as empty and hollow as a suit of armor—perhaps even a place of vacant possession for mischievous spirits. We should not, of course, blame Rowling as the messenger for bringing us the bad news. We should not even blame ourselves as Christians for having let the situation get so bad. We should, instead, concentrate on finding imaginative and inventive ways of helping people to learn the proper lyrics to the carols they happily sing, and of putting Christ back into the empty armor of Christmas. And here, strangely enough, Rowling is far more friend than foe.

GILDING THE LILY

The superficial vestiges of Christmas are not the only elements of the Christian faith to have made it into Potterworld. I do not know whether Joanne Rowling would consider herself to be a Christian or not, so I am not for one moment suggesting that she has "smuggled" Christian theology into her work in the way that, say, C. S. Lewis did. A couple of years after writing his Mars novel *Out of the Silent Planet*, and a decade before Narnia, he wrote to a friend, "Any amount of theology can be smuggled into people's minds under the cover of romance without their knowing it."[5] To be fair, Lewis never actually intended to put theology into his novels when he began writing them in his mind. "Everything began with images," he once explained; "a faun carrying an umbrella, a queen on a sledge, a magnificent lion. At first there wasn't even anything Christian about them; that element pushed itself in of its own accord. It was part of the bubbling."[6] However, once these characteristics had surfaced, he was not in the least ashamed of using them to communicate a message (provided they didn't become too twisted or artificial in the process). While Rowling might well share such an approach in handling morality— she seems happy to include fairly overt moral lessons in the books, provided they have arisen naturally as what Lewis called "part of the bubbling"—I suspect the snippets of traditional Christian theology that have smuggled themselves into Potterworld in various guises have done so very largely without her knowledge.

They are there, in other words, because they are "part of the bubbling" of our culture as a whole which Rowling picks up. That they are characteristically (if perhaps not exclusively) Christian seems almost accidental to her purpose. In much the same way that she probably called the wizards' hospital St. Mungo's Hospital for Magical Maladies and Injuries simply because she liked the name—rather than because she wanted to reflect the fact that hospitals per se are a Christian innovation dating back to the A.D. 300s, or to honor the real St. Mungo (a.k.a. St. Kentigern), bishop of Strathclyde in the late A.D. 500s—so she would appear to have built several key themes of Christian theology into the fabric of Potterworld because they seemed to her to be innately valuable, whether they were Christian or not.

The most obvious of these, of course, and the one that runs most deeply through the whole Potter series, is the theme of self-sacrificial love. It is a doctrine expounded most fully and vocally by Sirius Black at the end of *Azkaban*, when a squirming Wormtail explains that he had no choice but to disclose the whereabouts of Lily and James Potter, as Voldemort was threatening to kill him:

> *"THEN YOU SHOULD HAVE DIED!" roared Black. "DIED RATHER THAN BETRAY YOUR FRIENDS, AS WE WOULD HAVE DONE FOR YOU!"*[7]

The wording and context may be rather different but the sentiment is very much that of Jesus: "This is my commandment, that you love one another as I have loved you. No one has greater love than this, to lay down one's life for one's friends."[8] Jesus himself, of course, laid down his life not just for a narrowly defined group of "friends" but for the entire world, and generations of Christian martyrs followed his example, laying down their lives for their friends, their faith, their fellow believers and, above all, the Gospel.

The prime example of self-sacrificial love in Potterworld, however, is that of Harry's mum and dad, Lily and James Potter. Just why Voldemort was so determined to kill them, and why he felt the need to kill baby Harry, remains to be seen.[9] What is clear is not only that Lily and James Potter were willing to lay down their own lives for each other and as part of a final effort to save the life of their only son but that this "foolish sacrifice" (as Voldemort considers it)—particularly that of his mother, Lily—somehow immunized Harry against the otherwise fatal Avada Kedavra curse. As the newly arisen Lord Voldemort explains:

> *"His mother died in the attempt to save him—and unwittingly provided him with a protection I admit I had not foreseen . . . His mother left upon him the traces of her sacrifice . . . this is old magic, I should have remembered it."*[10]

What is more, the same self-sacrificial attitude can be found throughout the series in a whole host of characters. It is not just Padfoot Black and Moony Lupin who are willing to die rather than betray their friends—Harry, Ron and Hermione are constantly risking both life and limb for their comrades and the wider community, wizard and Muggle alike. From taking on a troll to tackling the terrors of the trapdoor, self-sacrifice is a frequent motif in *Sorcerer's Stone*, and it is no less present in *Chamber of Secrets*, where Ron and Harry brave the evils of the Heir and the Chamber in order to save the lives of Ginny and Hermione. If death is not always forthcoming, it is certainly never shied away from. In *Azkaban*, Harry goes one step farther, risking his life not just for Ron, Hermione, Black and Snape against the Dementors (who seem to be past the point of caring whether they take the innocent along with the guilty) but even for Wormtail, whose murder he prevents by putting himself physically in its way. In *Goblet of Fire*, Harry's self-sacrificial attitude develops even more: Harry risks attack from the merpeople and then suffocation in order to rescue all the hostages from the depths of the lake in his second Triwizard task; he risks literally *excruciating* torture in order to save

Cedric Diggory from an Imperiated Krum, and in order to save him again from the gigantic spider in his final task; and he risks his life once more dodging Voldemort's wand blasts in order to fulfill his promise and return Cedric's corpse to his distraught parents.

In fact Rowling appears to extol the virtues of self-sacrificial love not just in extremis but as a round-the-clock philosophy of life, complete with its own innate rewards. In *Goblet of Fire*, Harry's daring attempt to rescue all the water hostages is described as having "moral fiber" but the same fiber shows itself much earlier (and in less extreme circumstances) in his concern that Cedric should not be the only Triwizard champion ignorant of the dangers ahead, even though telling him about the dragons lessens Harry's own advantage.

The Potter books are replete with similar examples but it is *Azkaban* that gives us what is perhaps the clearest explanation to date of just *why* self-sacrificial love is considered such a vital virtue. When Harry prevents Padfoot and Moony from lynching Wormtail, he explains that he doesn't think his father would want his best friends to become murderers, and certainly not on his account. Harry is clear that he is prepared to prevent Wormtail's death, risking his own life, not because Wormtail is especially worth it—he never actually rejects Padfoot's harsh definition of him as a "cringing bit of filth"[11]— but because there is something essentially *ig*noble about murder and something essentially noble about mercy and self-sacrifice. In believing this, he echoes his father's will.

Rowling would seem to embrace self-sacrificial love as being something of a credo—a moral philosophy to live by. It is so closely woven into the fabric of Potterworld that we can only assume that it is a vital component not merely of what Tolkien would have called her Secondary World (Potterworld) but also of her Primary World (her life with her daughter in Edinburgh). She may not, for all we know, actually practice her creed any more successfully than we in the Church practice ours—as the joke goes, "The Church is *not* full of hypocrites: There's always room for one more!"—but it is at least a creed worth living by, and we find in it echoes of the uniquely Christian belief that our call to live (and die) for others is rooted in the fact that God, in the person of Jesus, lived and died for us.

"BLESSED ARE THE MERCIFUL . . ."

In Christian theology, the belief in self-sacrifice and mercy is intrinsically linked to the belief that we ourselves are the recipients of self-sacrifice and mercy. Mercy—both a motivator and a mechanism of self-sacrifice—involves taking on oneself the consequences, emotional and otherwise, of another person's wrongdoing. Those who are merciful are those who are more concerned about the welfare of others than about their own rights and requirements. They are, whether they understand this or not, investing their energies and resources (and sometimes, of course, their lives) in a virtuous circle of transformation. "Blessed are the merciful," declared Jesus, "for they will receive mercy."[12] True enough. But to a large extent, at least in terms of those reading the Gospels now, the "merciful" are those who have already received mercy. As Paul put it, "God proves his love for us in that while we were still sinners Christ died for us."[13] John reflects the same rich vein of thinking:

> *God's love was revealed among us in this way: God sent his only Son into the world so that we might live through him. In this is love, not that we loved God but that he loved us and sent his Son to be the atoning sacrifice for our sins. Beloved, since God loved us so much, we also ought to love one another.*[14]

From the perspective of Christian theology, therefore, self-sacrifice is not just the noble thing to do—it is the *Christian* thing to do, the *godly* thing to do, because it reflects the selfless love of God himself. In acting self-sacrificially, we follow the example of Christ and enable others to experience the redemption we ourselves have been given. This is the rationale that makes sense of otherwise paradoxical statements like, "Those who want to save their life will lose it, and those who lose their life for my sake will save it."[15]

There are intimations in Potterworld, as well, of the redemptive power of love (albeit without any reference to God). For an example of love transforming enemies into friends, we need to look, as we already have, at Harry, Hermione, Ron and the incident with the troll. For a view of the redeeming and transforming qualities of love, we might look at the relationship between Hagrid and Dumbledore. Expelled for nurturing the giant spider Aragog in the Hogwarts basement—a beast thought responsible for a death actually caused by the activities of Slytherin's basilisk, unleashed by Tom Riddle from the Chamber of Secrets—he is given a job in the Hogwarts grounds by Dumbledore's predecessor, Armando Dippet, at the behest of the school's Transfiguration teacher, Dumbledore himself. Hagrid's loyalty to Dumbledore subsequently knows no bounds. We may see him do no more than give Dudley Dursley a pink and curly pig's tail when Uncle Vernon dares to insult the "great man," but we are left in little doubt that he would not hesitate to lay down his life for Dumbledore if the need arose.

There is an element of risk involved, of course, but the investment generally pays off. Rather than joining the other giants in exile, Hagrid continues to live and work at Hogwarts, being promoted to Keeper of the Keys and playing a vital part in delivering baby Harry to the relative safety of his uncle and aunt's house. Taking risks is a policy that clearly characterizes Dumbledore: We are told by Black that he "trusts where a lot of other people wouldn't,"[16] and while this results in the occasional error of judgment—he fails adequately to notice the change in Quirrell, or to spot the substitution of the bogus Moody for the real one before the start of term, despite their long friendship—we know from Black's own experience, and that of the outcast teacher Remus Lupin, that it is generally wiser than its alternative. We see this especially at the end of *Goblet of Fire*, when he advises Fudge to send peace envoys to the giants before Voldemort is able to exploit their alienation from the wizard community and recruit them himself, as he did before. Dumbledore's rationale is simple: Make friends with the giants and there is a chance they will make friends with you; make enemies of the giants and there is a cast-iron certainty they will make enemies of you. The risk involved in trusting the giants is less than the risk involved in *not* trusting them, and leaving them to Voldemort.

But risk is an essential part of redemption—an essential element of the Christian Gospel. The old story about Jesus at heaven's gate has a ring of truth to it: After his ascension, Jesus comes with the clouds of heaven and arrives at heaven's gate, where he is met by an angel. The angel looks down at the fledgling pre-Pentecost Church and asks, "What will you do if it doesn't work?" Jesus replies, "I have no other plan." The salvation of the whole world rests precariously at that moment in the hands of a few dozen frightened men and women whose track record is less than encouraging. It is a risky endeavor but one God is willing to take. Human freedom inevitably involves risk, just as it inevitably involves gradual change and learning (and even a lot of mistakes) rather than instant perfection, but the risk is worth it.

In Christian theology, of course, it is specifically *God's* love that unleashes and enables the transformation of people. In this, we might note, it is quite different from the idea of redemption displayed in

Rowling's characters. As we have already noted, there seemingly *is* no God in Potterworld—not a knowable one, at any rate. What we are seeing in the Harry Potter saga, therefore, is a kind of *secular* and *humanist* process of redemption—of one character unleashing and enabling the gradual transformation of another.

This is, of course, quite true. However, the same accusation could easily be leveled at Lewis's Narnia. It may indeed be Aslan whose self-sacrificial act of love transforms Edmund (although he is already disenchanted with the Witch by this point) in *The Lion, the Witch and the Wardrobe*; who frees Eustace from his dragon's skin in *The Voyage of the Dawn Treader;* who emboldens Jill in *The Silver Chair* and Shasta in *The Horse and His Boy* to go on to save Narnia from the threat of invasion; and who sets Digory straight in *The Magician's Nephew*. Nevertheless, only those readers who are able, and knowledgable enough, to understand and correctly interpret Lewis's allegory will make a connection between Aslan and Jesus, and most Narnia readers—aged roughly between seven and twelve (though the books are not actually targeted at readers under nine)—are too young to manage this. In other words, to children Narnia is no more explicit about the idea that Jesus is the ultimate redeemer and that God's love engenders our own than Potterworld. What is more, in Narnia as in Harry Potter, one character (often having been affected by Aslan) goes on to help the transformation of another: Edmund helps Eustace, Eustace helps Jill, Jill helps Puddleglum, and so on. Both Lewis and Rowling use the love of one character to bring about the redemption and transformation of another. To put it another way—one more couched in the language of Christian theology— both Lewis and Rowling depict their gospel of love being transmitted by human evangelists, who preach their message as much with their lives as with their words.

Theologically, we must be wary of writing off acts of love, self-sacrifice and mercy as "ungodly" merely because God remains unmentioned. The love of God is at work by his Spirit acting in the world even when human beings refuse to acknowledge him. Our blindness does not invalidate his presence. Moreover, if—as Christians claim—each person is made in the image of God, it follows that however marred and blighted that image may be, God somehow is at work. The love, compassion and mercy shown by human beings to one another do not arise from autonomous human nature, however much humanists believe they do. Rather, they are the reflections of God, and as such we should welcome them in fiction as well as in fact.

REDEEMED BY THE BLOOD?

The nonreligious narrative of redemption in Potterworld gives rise to an interesting and critical question which has its parallel in Christian theology: Is there no end to redemption and to who might be redeemed? What about Voldemort? Is there any chance for him?

The realistic answer to this is probably not. He may once have risen to be Head Boy of Hogwarts—a star pupil and recipient of an award for special services to the school—but we know from *Chamber of Secrets* that his clean-cut reputation was a facade that came at the expense of those such as Hagrid, who was expelled for supposedly having opened the Chamber and released the basilisk, actions for which Voldemort himself was responsible. Even before his descent into real evil, he was determined to match and even exceed the notoriety of Salazar Slytherin (who had, after all, worked with Gryffindor, Hufflepuff and Ravenclaw for long enough to found Hogwarts), and proved himself able to kill (literally) in cold blood.

"He disappeared after leaving the school . . . traveled far and wide . . . sank so deeply into the Dark Arts, consorted with the very worst of our kind, underwent so many dangerous, magical transformations, that when he resurfaced as Lord Voldemort, he was barely recognizable. Hardly anyone connected Lord Voldemort with the clever, handsome boy who was once Head Boy here."[17]

To ask if Voldemort can be saved is therefore to ask basically the same question of the devil. Our instinctive answer is to say that he is beyond redemption. But there remains a hesitation in Voldemort's case, for there is a tantalizing possibility left open by Rowling—a possibility that Voldemort will indeed be saved from his own innate evil, though the likelihood is rather that it speaks of his eventual defeat. When Harry tells Dumbledore that Voldemort used his blood as part of the spell to make him arise, he explains, "He said the protection my—my mother left in me—he'd have it, too. And he was right—he could touch me without hurting himself, he touched my face." Dumbledore's reaction is odd: "For a fleeting instant, Harry thought he saw a gleam of something like triumph in Dumbledore's eyes."[18] Could Voldemort really be undone, or perhaps even redeemed, in the final installment of the Potter saga by the "powerful countercharm" of the self-sacrificial love of Lily Potter coursing through his callous veins by means of her son's blood? It is an intriguing idea.

A colleague of mine, an expert in the Levitical laws of the Old Testament, was once quoted by his students as having said, "You can do all sorts of things with blood." Although it sounds macabre, his point is that blood functioned in Old Testament times as a kind of "black box." In technological terms, this is a device that can be successfully used by people who have no idea how it actually works—we can use a car to get around without any real understanding of the inner workings of the internal combustion engine, for example. In the same way, blood symbolized and brought about redemption for the people of ancient Israel even if they didn't fully understand why. In fact understanding why is far from easy, and this book is certainly not the place to explain it in any kind of detail. However, Rowling's inclusion of a blood rite in *Goblet of Fire* makes it appropriate briefly to examine three perspectives on the efficacy of blood, death and sacrifice to be found in Potterworld.

The first perspective is that of *propitiation* (a term used positively with a significantly different meaning in traditional Christian theology). In most cultures, sacrifice probably arose from a belief that gods, like people, needed feeding, and that those who gave them what they needed would please them and might in turn be given a reward. From this grew the idea that sacrifice could be propitiatory—it could be used to appease a god, turning aside its anger. One of the best examples of this idea is found in William Golding's novel *The Lord of the Flies*. When their plane crash-lands, a group of boys is stranded on a deserted island with no grown-ups. What starts as paradise soon turns nasty, however, as the boys' fears run away with them. Frightened by the darkness of the island at night, and the fact that at least one of their number has disappeared without trace, they begin to believe in the existence of a dreadful island beast. At first, they are simply afraid of the beast but their fear then drives them to make sacrifices to it, convinced that if they can only assuage its anger and satisfy its hunger, it will leave them alone. The first sacrifices are choice portions of the wild pigs they have killed for food but by the end of the book, when bitter infighting has led to violent clashes between rival factions, and fear has spiraled out of control, the beast is given its first taste of human sacrifice as well. In Potterworld, propitiation gets its clearest expression (though the word is never mentioned) in

Crouch the Younger's desire to finish what Voldemort started by killing Harry at the end of *Goblet of Fire*. Fear mingles with the desire to please, with murderous intent:

> *"The Dark Lord didn't manage to kill you, Potter, and he so wanted to, " whispered Moody. "Imagine how he will reward me, when he finds I have done it for him. I gave you to him—the thing he needed above all to re-generate—and then I killed you for him. I will be honored beyond all other Death Eaters. "*[19]

The second perspective is that of *magic*. Crucial to both this view and the next is the ancient observation that an animal's life was carried in its blood—drain the blood and it dies. What is more, for many ancient cultures, an animal or person's *strength* was also carried in its blood. From the perspective of imitative magic, therefore, if you consumed an animal, and especially its blood, you took into yourself its strength and character. Rather gruesomely, for some cultures this was equally true of other humans: Eat your enemies, for example, and you added their strength and courage to your own. One reason why God in Leviticus specifically prohibited the Israelites from eating meat with blood still in it, therefore, was to banish this kind of magical thinking completely. (Another reason is that, as its life, a creature's blood was judged to belong to its creator God alone.) We see this magical perspective in Voldemort's desire to use Harry's blood in the potion that revives him:

> *"Wormtail would have had me use any wizard, would you not, Wormtail? Any wizard who had hated me . . . as so many of them still do. But I knew the one I must use, if I was to rise again, more powerful than I had been when I had fallen. I wanted Harry Potter's blood. I wanted the blood of the one who had stripped me of power thirteen years ago, for the*

lingering protection his mother once gave him, would then reside in my veins, too . . ."[20]

The third perspective—the only one of the three to be viewed positively in Potterworld—is that of *atonement*. As God explains to the Israelites in Leviticus, "The life of the flesh is in the blood; and I have given it to you for making atonement for your lives on the altar; for, as life, it is the blood that makes atonement."[21] Here my colleague's "black box" theory comes into its own, as we don't actually have to know the exact mechanics of *how* blood achieves atonement in order for it to do so. As theologian Howard Marshall has suggested, even the New Testament writers themselves were "more concerned with the nature of salvation than the precise way in which it has been achieved."[22] Both atonement and the "black box" approach to it seem to be part of Potterworld as well. Just why Lily Potter's self-sacrificial death should have saved her son from the deadly Avada Kedavra curse and affected his blood is never properly explained; but we are left in no doubt that this *has* happened.

In many ways, Rowling has plugged into an idea that runs deep in our culture, defined by Christian theology but no longer restricted to it. Just as Christmas is now by and large a post-Christian celebration, so there remains in our culture a profound identification with the idea of atonement, and its connection with blood, even though our knowledge of, and interest in, the Christian theology that spawned this concept is now all but gone. Rowling sees and reflects an innate value in atonement even though it is detached from its true theological roots. Though there is no God figure in Potterworld for anyone to be made *at one*[23] with, the idea that the death of one person can save another— at a mystical level, not simply a practical one—emerges as what C. S. Lewis would call "part of the bubbling." She may use magic as a convenient "black box" to avoid explaining just how an atoning sacrifice works and what it does (in the same way that Lewis uses "deeper magic" as a "black box" in *The Lion, the Witch and the Wardrobe* to avoid explaining the mechanics of the atoning death of Aslan) but its effectiveness is not diminished by this shorthand. Whatever Rowling had in mind when she introduced the concept of atonement into Potterworld, we connect with it (whether we have a church affiliation or not) because it is a rich vein running deep within our culture.

THE UNDISCOVER'D COUNTRY

Christian theology, of course, cannot talk for long about atonement and redemption without referring to death and resurrection. In contemporary culture the idea of resurrection has little meaning. But there persists a notion of the afterlife; and it is here perhaps where Potterworld reflects most accurately the uncertainties of modern belief. But it is also the place where Christian thinking and the theological framework of Potterworld are most at odds.

With no ostensible God, Potterworld has little in the way of traditional ideas about "heaven" and "hell" let alone resurrection. There is no real equivalent of heaven in the Potter books—nowhere for the "souls of the faithful departed" to "rest in peace" and no obvious locus of the afterlife in which Harry, for example, can be reunited with his parents. The closest Rowling gets to imagining hell is the wizard island prison Azkaban, with its evil Dementor wardens, which she has repeatedly suggested draws its inspiration (if you can call it that) from her own experience of the debilitating effects of chronic depression.

"Dementors are among the foulest creatures that walk this earth. They infest the darkest, filthiest places, they glory in decay and despair, they drain peace, hope and happiness out of the air around them. Even

Muggles feel their presence, though they can't see them. Get too near a Dementor and every good feeling, every happy memory, will be sucked out of you. If it can, the Dementor will feed on you long enough to reduce you to something like itself—soulless and evil."[24]

Rowling is, it would seem, largely uninterested in speculating about the afterlife, good or bad, and includes references only to those elements of it that immediately impact on Harry and his friends in the land of the living. It is not entirely missing from Potterworld but what there is has its anchor firmly in *this* world, not the next. Hogwarts has its fair share of ghosts, for a start. Its houses even have patron ghosts, the way some schools or schoolhouses have patron saints: Gryffindor's jovial Nearly Headless Nick, for example, or Slytherin's sinister Bloody Baron. Ghosts, we are told, return to haunt the land of the living when there is a strong tether to hold them there. Moaning Myrtle, for instance, died after seeing Slytherin's basilisk but returned because she was "determined to haunt Olive Hornby," who had bullied her when she was still alive.[25] Professor Binns, the dead boring History of Magic teacher, "had been very old indeed when he had fallen asleep in front of the staff room fire and got up the next morning to teach, leaving his body behind him."[26]

Some form of postmortem existence, though again more literary than philosophical, also seems to be evident in the effects of Priori Incantatem, "the reverse spell effect," which occurs when the twin wands of Harry and Voldemort—twinned because they each contain at their core a single feather from Dumbledore's phoenix, Fawkes—are made to fight each other and thereby "force the other to regurgitate spells it has performed—in reverse," leading to the emergence of the "reverse echoes" of Voldemort's victims.[27] Cedric Diggory, Frank Bryce and Bertha Jorkins emerge just as they died, as if no time had passed (though with a greater ability to recognize the reality of their situation) but Harry's dad not only emerges *before* his mum (rather than after, as the reversing effect should have made happen) but seems to be aware of what she will say and do: " 'Your mother's coming . . .' he said quietly. 'She wants to see you . . . it will be all right . . . hold on . . .' "[28] This is, no doubt, dramatic license, and anyway does not represent a true afterlife. Nevertheless, together with the presence of ghosts it hints that perhaps death might not, after all, be the absolute end.

For Albus Dumbledore and his former alchemy partner, Nicholas Flamel, it certainly is not. When Flamel discovers the alchemic Sorcerer's Stone, source of an Elixir of Life that bestows immortality on those who continue to drink it, he and his wife face the prospect of never having to die. When it becomes clear, however, that Voldemort will stop at nothing to acquire the Stone and its Elixir in order to attain immortality for himself, and Flamel decides to destroy it rather than allow it to fall into the wrong hands, he once more joins the realm of the mortals. Dumbledore, however, denies that this is really a tragedy:

> *"After all, to the well-organized mind, death is but the next great adventure. You know, the Stone was really not such a wonderful thing. As much money and life as you could want! The two things most human beings would choose above all—the trouble is, humans do have a knack of choosing precisely those things which are worst for them."*[29]

The suggestion that death can be an adventure rather than necessarily a disaster does perhaps seem to hint at the idea that there *is* something after it—what Shakespeare's Hamlet called "the undiscover'd country from whose bourn no traveller returns."[30] Rowling may not specify what this might be but the suggestion itself is enticing and, for Christian readers, most welcome.

Dumbledore's comment does, however, raise a further issue—a criticism, really, of both Voldemort and some traditional views of heaven. Longevity, he suggests, is "really not such a wonderful thing." Voldemort, aware that "no spell can reawaken the dead,"[31] and keen to ensure that his power goes on forever, goes to enormous lengths to make himself immortal, which finally explains how he manages to survive the ricochet of his seemingly fatal curse:

"I was ripped from my body, I was less than spirit, less than the meanest ghost . . . but still, I was alive. What I was, even I do not know . . . I, who have gone further than anybody along the path that leads to immortality. You know my goal—to conquer death. And now, I was tested, and it appeared that one or more of my experiments had worked . . . for I had not been killed, though the curse should have done it."[32]

But have all his experiments really been worth it? What has Voldemort *achieved* by cheating death? His insane will to power has certainly not been sated and the ordeal of acquiring even partial immortality—especially if what he calls his "experiments" are what Dumbledore called the "dangerous, magical transformations" that made him "barely recognizable"[33]—appears to have robbed him of those qualities we would, along with the prophet Micah, consider basic to being human: justice, kindness and humility before God.[34] In his bid to live forever, the Dark Lord has lost the point of living at all.

The same can be said of those for whom the idea of the afterlife is fundamentally to do with the *length* of life rather than its *quality*. Lewis was wise at the end of *The Last Battle* to present heaven in terms of a garden in which dimensions of time and space no longer have the same hold or importance they did before, and in which joy and relationships are paramount. It is hardly coincidental, I think, that those Potterworld characters who are most afraid of death—and we are *all* afraid of it to some extent, no matter how firmly we believe in what is to come afterward—and who would stoop to any level rather than face it square on, are those who have abandoned the joys and honest relationships of life, and have embraced instead the dark side of magic. If magic really is, as I suggested in Chapter One, a symbol of power—it was, after all, in those societies where magic was common (and occasionally still is), an attempt to manipulate either the gods or nature, or both, for personal or social gain—then this simply becomes all the more appropriate. Voldemort and his supporters are driven by their own fears to use all the power at their disposal, no matter whom it harms, to put off the inevitable, and in the process they lose sight of the essential.

But, for all this, we find ourselves returning once more to what is missing, namely the central truth that sets Christianity apart—the promise of resurrection. The reader will search in vain for any mention of it. Resurrection is simply not part of the Potter worldview. We should not be surprised at this any more than we should be shocked by the omission of any reference to the doctrine of the Trinity. Rowling has not written the Potter series as a collection of religious tracts or (unlike Lewis) as a religious allegory. The most we can hope for are some echoes of Christian truths at various points. Theology is present in Potterworld but it is partial and muted, more implicit than explicit. We should not judge its author too harshly—she does not set out to be a theologian—and we should not expect too much. But, as we have seen, although not couched in the language of theology, the reader *is* presented with some profound theological ideas—and for that we should be glad.

chapter five

THE JOURNEY FROM PLATFORM NINE AND THREE-QUARTERS

THE METAPHYSICS OF POTTERWORLD

"I just take the train from platform nine and three-quarters at eleven o'clock," he read.
His aunt and uncle stared.
"Platform what?"
"Nine and three-quarters."
"Don't talk rubbish," said Uncle Vernon,
"there is no platform nine and three-quarters."
"It's on my ticket."[1]

To read Harry Potter requires a huge act of faith. It requires us to suspend our cherished belief that the world around us is the only possible kind of reality there could be and to accept that, in the imagination at least, there could be another. What is more, by its very nature, Potterworld asks us to switch off our rational circuits—those parts of our brains that tell us that what we're reading simply can't be happening—and to enter a universe in which the normal laws of nature are overtaken by an alternate reality which is somehow capable of impossible feats. We all *know* that people can't really turn themselves into animals, that giants and dragons don't actually exist, and that there's no such thing as platform nine and three-quarters at London's King's Cross Station but we decide to believe in these things in spite of what we know so that we can enjoy the books on their own terms. Those who can't or won't allow their imaginations free reign will inevitably dismiss Harry Potter as mere "nonsense" or "child's play."

This is a shame, because *all* fiction actually involves our suspending disbelief to some extent or another. Even the most grittily realistic of thrillers requires us to accept people and circumstances that don't actually exist, however plausible and otherwise convincing their plot lines and characterizations might be. It is in the nature of fiction that we're expected to accept things that aren't part of reality. Some stories stick quite closely to what we know, requiring only a small amount of disbelief to be suspended. Others, like Harry Potter, oblige us to take giant leaps into the unknown and accept more or less on face value things we know full well are *not* part of our day-to-day reality.

In this Harry Potter's magical environment is very similar to that of some of the most enduringly popular and respected works of literature through the ages—from the gods and monsters of the ancient Greek poet Homer in his *Iliad* and *Odyssey*, through the deities and devils of Chaucer's *Canterbury Tales* and the ghosts and goblins of Shakespeare's plays, to the wizards and weird creatures of Terry Pratchett's recent Discworld novels. Homer's initial audience may well have believed in the existence and reality of gods like Zeus and Hera or monstrous beings such as Scylla and Charybdis, but that doesn't mean they thought they were listening to real-time historical *reportage*—the ancient equivalent of CNN—whenever they heard his hexameters read aloud. They knew he was spinning a yarn and were happy to play along in order to enjoy it. In much the same way, Pratchett's readers are prepared to dispense with everyday reality for the duration of his books, even though they obviously harbor no illusions that the Discworld—a flat earth balanced atop four elephants traveling through space on the shell of a giant turtle—actually exists.

TO DREAM THE IMPOSSIBLE DREAM

It does, however, beg the question: Why? Why do we enjoy reading and hearing stories about events that not only have not happened but cannot happen? Why was by far the most popular English-language novel of the twentieth century a tale of epic fantasy: *The Lord of the Rings*? Is it pure escapism? Do we read and dream of things that cannot happen in order not to have to face the dreariness and seeming hopelessness of what does happen, day in and day out, in our own lives? Has fantasy literature like *The Lord of the Rings* and Harry Potter become, as Marx once said of religion, "the opium of the people"?[2]

Facing allegations of escapism head-on in 1938, after the publication of *The Hobbit*, Tolkien argued that if fantasy and fairy stories *were* escapist, the real problem wasn't so much the fantasy as the reality that people so clearly felt a need to escape from. "Why should a man be scorned if, finding himself in prison, he tries to get out and go home? Or if, when he cannot do so, he thinks and talks about other topics than jailers and prison walls?"[3]

For many of us, this kind of "escape" can play a very different role: not so much an opiate as a stimulant—something that provides our souls and imaginations with the impetus, inspiration and energy we need not just to *survive* our reality but to *transform* it. As we saw in

Chapter Two, fantasy literature can act as a spur to action—stories of flying carpets or broomsticks helped to create the atmosphere of expectation in which airplanes were made, and tales of space travel made the first moonshot conceivable. But, of course, fantasy need not be so directly related to what it produces. The point is not that fantasy writing *predicts* scientific or technological advances but that it stimulates our imaginations in such a way that we are encouraged to find new ways of imaging and understanding the world, rather than simply taking things at face value.

In fact imagination and a refusal to take things at face value play a big part in scientific understanding and discovery. If necessity is the *mother* of invention, then imagination must surely be its *father*. The ability to take an imaginative leap beyond accepted scientific dogma and the entrenched views of colleagues and apparent common sense, has been at the heart of a significant number of scientific or technological advances in the last few hundred years, even those that seem to be based on objective fact or cold hard logic. In the words of the physicist Max Planck, "New ideas are not generated by deduction but by an artistically creative imagination . . . Science, like the humanities, like literature, is an affair of the imagination."[4]

By encouraging her readers to imagine a world in which hard science is not all there is, J. K. Rowling has made it possible and legitimate to question whether the scientism of the Enlightenment must be taken at face value. This is a welcome development since, in all too many sectors of our society, "science" is seen as being little short of infallible—as having all the answers. As a result generations have grown up with the assumption that anything else must be dismissed as mere fancy.

Potterworld's anything-but-rational complement of hidden platforms, enchanted cars, Portkeys, Time-Turners, Whomping Willows,

Invisibility Cloaks and flying broomsticks will help the current generation of readers to develop the kind of imaginative skepticism that stops
them from taking things simply at face value, and probe more deeply. It
will keep them from turning into an Uncle Vernon, who, we are told,
after encountering the strange and unexpected in the form of Dedalus
Diggle, "Hurried to his car and set off home, hoping he was imagining
things, which he had never hoped before, because he didn't approve of
imagination."[5]

"I BELIEVE . . . HELP MY UNBELIEF"

Aside from Quidditch's flying broomsticks, of course, the first and
most obvious phenomenon to examine in looking at Potterworld's
metaphysics—its understanding of reality—is platform nine and
three-quarters. Like so much that concerns the interaction between
the Muggle world and the magical world in the Potter books, it is both
there and not there.

When Uncle Vernon drops Harry at King's Cross Station, he
sneers with cruel delight at the idea of Harry taking a magical train
from a nonexistent platform. Harry is at this point still quite naïve—
having been told by his letter to catch the Hogwarts Express from
there, it has simply never occurred to him that there is anything out of
the ordinary about having a platform numbered nine and three-
quarters. Only when he is left standing between platforms nine and
ten does he begin to realize his predicament:

> *"Well, there you are, boy. Platform nine—platform ten. Your platform
> should be somewhere in the middle, but they don't seem to have built it
> yet, do they?"*

He was quite right, of course. There was a big plastic number nine over one platform and a big plastic number ten over the one next to it, and in the middle, nothing at all.

"Have a good term," said Uncle Vernon with an even nastier smile. He left without another word. Harry turned and saw the Dursleys drive away. All three of them were laughing.[6]

However, in the space of just two pages of text, Harry moves right across the spectrum from childish naïveté, through healthy skepticism, to genuine belief when Molly Weasley and her troupe of red-headed children come to the rescue:

"Not to worry," she said. "All you have to do is walk straight at the barrier between platforms nine and ten. Don't stop and don't be scared you'll crash into it, that's very important. Best do it at a bit of a run if you're nervous. Go on, go now before Ron."

"Er—OK," said Harry.

He pushed his trolley round and stared at the barrier. It looked very solid.

He started to walk towards it. People jostled him on their way to platforms nine and ten. Harry walked more quickly. He was going to smash right into that ticket box and then he'd be in trouble—leaning forward on his trolley he broke into a heavy run—the barrier was coming nearer and nearer—he wouldn't be able to stop—the trolley was out of control—he was a foot away—he closed his eyes ready for the crash—

It didn't come . . . he kept on running . . . he opened his eyes.

A scarlet steam engine was waiting next to a platform packed with people. A sign overhead said Hogwarts Express, 11 o'clock. *Harry looked behind him and saw a wrought-iron archway where the ticket box had been, with the words* Platform Nine and Three-Quarters *on it. He had done it.*[7]

This same progression, from naïveté to skepticism to belief, is one that all of us follow in our efforts to understand the exact nature of the world about us—although as this ticket barrier incident suggests, skepticism and belief usually continue to go hand in hand rather than following one another in strict chronological order. (It might almost be said that skepticism and faith are alternate sides of the same coin.) Mrs. Weasley warns Harry not to be scared that he'll simply crash into the barrier—"that's very important," she explains, and we could be forgiven for imagining therefore that total and absolute belief is essential for getting through the magic—Muggle divide and onto the platform. Yet Harry does not have total and absolute belief. Having come close to panic because, with just ten minutes to go before the Hogwarts Express is due to leave the station, he still has no idea at all where platform nine and three-quarters actually is, he scrunches up his eyes and dashes toward the ticket barrier. If he had been a "true believer," filled with nothing but belief, Harry would not have "closed his eyes ready for the crash." At the same time, if he had had merely skepticism, he would never even have *tried* to cross the threshold onto the magical platform.

As strange as it seems, belief is an important part of both scientific and metaphysical processes. We tend to see science, at least, as something based on pure objective observation but faith is actually an essential part of its method. Scientists generally work by means of experimentation, and all experiments begin with an hypothesis. For the purpose and duration of the experiment, a scientist *believes* this: $x + y = z$, for example. They assume it to be correct, and act accordingly, adding x to y and looking for z in result. To the extent that the experiment supports the assumption, they can continue to believe it; otherwise, it is back to the drawing board. Metaphysics—the scholarly attempt to understand the nature of reality—works in just the same way: Where practical experiments aren't possible, a theory is tested by trying to think through what all the consequences would be if it *were* true, and comparing that with the way things appear to be. In both cases, nothing is achieved or ascertained by merely speculating from the sidelines—a certain level of committed involvement is necessary. As St. Anselm, the eleventh-century philosopher and Archbishop of Canterbury, put it, "I do not seek to understand so that I may believe, but I believe so that I may understand."[8]

But a healthy dose of skepticism is equally necessary. The physicist Richard Feynman used to warn his students that when they did research, and before publishing their results, they should think of every possible way in which they might be wrong. Another physicist, Alan Lightman, explains the vital importance of this: "In science, as in other activities, there is a tendency to find what we're looking for."[9] If Harry and Ron's mad rush onto platform nine and three-quarters illustrates the belief required to test a scientific hypothesis, then their cast-iron certainty of Professor Snape's guilt in *Sorcerer's Stone* illustrates the dangers of not tempering belief with skepticism. Snape's questionable past, his outright hatred of Harry, his magical interference during the Gryffindor—Slytherin Quidditch match and his insistence on refereeing the following match with Hufflepuff, his hushed conversations with Quirrell—all of these add up, in the minds of Harry, Ron and Hermione, to a clear indication of his intent to steal the Stone and return his former master to power. They add up quite wrongly, of course: The trio fail to ask themselves what *alternative* interpretations could be put on the evidence.

THE OPEN SECRET

Not taking things at face value is one of the cardinal virtues of Potterworld. In moral terms, we saw this very much in Chapter

Three. In physical and metaphysical terms, we see it perhaps most clearly in the apparent invisibility of the wizard world to Muggles. Rowling ascribes this to two causes: Enchantments to make wizarding phenomena either fade into the background or appear to be something quite different to what they really are, and Muggle unwillingness to recognize or investigate anything truly out of the ordinary.

On the first count—enchantments—Rowling provides us with abundant evidence of things either misseeming or being made magically invisible or unnoticeable. The easiest way to make something invisible is, of course, just to throw an Invisibility Cloak like Harry's over it but as this is not always possible—or perhaps desirable, as what lies beneath an Invisibility Cloak cannot be seen even by other wizards (we can only assume, for Rowling does not say, that the cloak becomes invisible only when someone is underneath it; otherwise you could never see it to put it on)—other methods must be employed. Nine times out of ten this means hiding something in plain sight by magically disguising it or, as in the case of platform nine and three-quarters or the wizard shopping "high street" of Diagon Alley, altering its physical dimensions and folding space in on itself (as famously happens with Dr. Who's Tardis). The Ministry of Magic's cars in *Azkaban*, for example, are described as anonymous-looking but since they seem capable of warping space around them in order to squeeze through gaps that a normal car would not manage, we can only assume that they are also bewitched with charms that make them invisible to Muggle drivers.

Hogwarts is equally bewitched to appear transfigured to the Muggle eye. A remote rural location in Scotland clearly doesn't provide it with enough security and obscurity, especially in this day and age of detailed aerial and satellite surveillance and photography, so the school, as Hermione explains to Harry and Ron ("Honestly, am I the *only* person who's ever bothered to read *Hogwarts, A History*?"),[10] comes equipped with other precautionary devices, not only to stop wizards Apparating within its walls but to stop Muggles from noticing it:

> *"It's bewitched," said Hermione. "If a Muggle looks at it, all they see is a moldering old ruin with a sign over the entrance saying DANGER, DO NOT ENTER, UNSAFE."*[11]

The alternative, she continues, would be to hide it with the kind of Muggle-Repelling Charms that cover every inch of the massive and imposing Quidditch World Cup stadium. As Arthur Weasley notes, "Every time Muggles have got anywhere near here all year, they've suddenly remembered urgent appointments and had to dash away again."[12] Things can even be made Unplottable: "You can enchant a building so it's impossible to plot on a map."[13] If things go wrong, a person's memory of what they have seen can be suppressed using a Memory Charm, though this is not only morally questionable because of its invasiveness, but also dangerous in terms of its ability either to fail (as in the case of campsite owner Mr. Roberts) or to cause permanent memory damage (as in the case of Bertha Jorkins).

From a theological perspective it is worth noting that by introducing the combination of skepticism and faith together, Rowling has (perhaps unwittingly) made a shrewd point about the nature of our quest for truth. Hard science of the Englightenment sort refused to concede that truth could be found in anything that could not be indubitably proven. This effectively consigned everything except that which could be demonstrated empirically to the category of mere opinion or fancy. The metaphysics of Potterworld, however, offers a different view. Truth and reality may be found beyond the obvious physical realm and it is possible that the two realms might coexist, even if we are not aware of it. There is much here to be welcomed by Christians, who have been making the same point for millennia.

THE PHILOSOPHY OF THE MUNDANE

One of the reasons, however, for the observational incompetence of Potterworld is that we Muggles fail to see magical phenomena, both because we do not *expect* to see them and because, frankly, we do not *want* to see them. They make us question reality, and that is not something we are at all keen to do. We are not natural metaphysicians.

In the pseudonymous *Fantastic Beasts & Where to Find Them*, Rowling explores this idea at greater length with reference to "magical and monstrous creatures." Although a considerable amount of effort has to be maintained at all times by national and international magical organizations to ensure that magical beasts remain largely undetected by Muggles, this, she explains, was not always the case.

> *A glance through Muggle art and literature of the Middle Ages reveals that many of the creatures they now believe to be imaginary were then known to be real. The dragon, the griffin, the unicorn, the phoenix, the centaur—these and more are represented in Muggle works of that period, though usually with almost comical inexactitude.*[14]

Only since the era of the Enlightenment, in other words, and the rise of rationalism—with its rigid view of a nature governed by intractable rules and straitjacketed by very clear ideas of just what is and is not physically possible—has it been necessary for wizards to conceal the existence of fantastic beasts. Before then, they were either accepted (though Rowling makes no mention of this, the Authorized

Version of the Bible, first published in 1611, refers several times to the unicorn)[15] or killed (dragons, for example, were often hunted in the Dark Ages), or else they escaped notice altogether. The rise of a more empirical mind-set, however, forced a summit meeting of the International Confederation of Wizards in 1692, in which certain species of fantastic beast were given protected status.

The implicit suggestion in all this, of course, is that the rational categories we generally use to determine what *is* and *is not* possible (in this case, what kind of creature can and cannot exist) do not always fit the facts. When the two clash, however, we would far rather ignore or subconsciously alter any disturbing evidence to ensure it fits our rigid categories than alter our rigid categories to ensure they fit the disturbing evidence. Aided and abetted by the Office of Misinformation, we opt for the first plausible, nonmagical explanation going:

> *There can be no doubt that the overwhelming majority of present-day Muggles refuse to believe in the magical beasts that their ancestors so feared. Even those Muggles who do notice Porlock droppings or Streeler trails—it would be foolish to suppose that all traces of these creatures can be hidden—appear satisfied with the flimsiest non-magical explanation.*[16]

For Rowling, our desire not to have our concept of reality disturbed or altered seems to be behind our reluctance to confront the unexpected or unthinkable, as well as our willingness to bend over backward and do cartwheels to believe something utterly *improbable* in order not to have to review our definitions of what is and is not *impossible*. She dubs this reluctance the "Philosophy of the Mundane":

> *For a fascinating examination of this fortunate tendency of Muggles, the reader might like to consult* The Philosophy of the Mundane: Why

the Muggles Prefer Not to Know, *Professor Mordicus Egg (Dust & Mildewe, 1963).* [17]

I do not for one moment imagine that Joanne Rowling herself actually believes in the physical reality of unicorns and centaurs (or even Porlocks and Steelers) any more than you or I do—or, for that matter, any more than did Lewis, whose Narnia books featured both of these fantastic beasts (and a good many others besides), and who similarly constructed his narrative in order gently to ridicule those who were unwilling to accept them even in literary form. Nor do I think that child readers will actually believe in the physical reality of such magical and monstrous creatures. Aside from their sheer entertainment value, and the considerable amount of fun to be had with them in *Fantastic Beasts*, the reason for Rowling including them—and magic in general—in her stories is not to indoctrinate children to imagine that fairies, pixies, gnomes, leprechauns and trolls, for example, genuinely exist but to encourage them to keep a more open mind on the nature of reality. As we noted in Chapter Two, Rowling suggested that the starting point for Harry Potter was the question, What if the magical and fantastic elements were *real*? What if there actually *were* dragons, goblins, flying broomsticks and magic spells? In a way, this very metaphysical question is the raison d'être of Potterworld. Its view of reality is open-minded. "There are more things in heaven and earth," as Shakespeare's Hamlet tells Horatio, "than are dreamt of in your philosophy." [18]

At the heart of science is an open mind but all too often in our society "science" is used to justify exactly the opposite approach: a closed-minded bigotry that decides before an experiment is even carried out just what kind of potential results are intellectually acceptable and what are not, regardless of any evidence the experiment itself actually provides to the contrary. This was the approach of those learned experts who opposed Galileo's heliocentric "fancy" on principle, for example: They had already decided a priori on philosophical grounds that Copernicus' earlier heliocentric ideas *could not* be correct, and *could not* be supported by Galileo's recent observational evidence before reading even a single word of the old Italian's controversial *Dialogue on the Two Chief World Systems*. But it is also the approach of many of those learned experts today who oppose all talk of miracles on principle: They have already decided a priori on supposedly "scientific" grounds that miracles *cannot* happen and *cannot* be supported by any evidence that might seem to show the contrary.

In Potterworld, where magic displaces miracles, we see this prejudicial approach in, of all people, the ghostly Professor Binns in *Chamber of Secrets*. When Hermione raises a hand to ask him a question midlesson, the Hogwarts History of Magic teacher is so taken aback at being interrupted (which seemingly has never happened before) that he humors her request and gives the class some of the historical background to what he calls the "very *sensational*, even *ludicrous* tale" of the Chamber. When he has finished explaining what all the historical sources recount, he makes his own view of the subject very clear:

> "*These honest facts have been obscured by the fanciful legend of the Chamber of Secrets. The story goes that Slytherin had built a hidden chamber in the castle, of which the other founders knew nothing.*
>
> "*Slytherin, according to the legend, sealed the Chamber of Secrets so that none would be able to open it until his own true heir arrived at the school. The heir alone would be able to unseal the Chamber of Secrets, unleash the horror within, and use it to purge the school of all who were unworthy to study magic . . .*

> *"The whole thing is arrant nonsense, of course," he said. "Naturally the school has been searched for evidence of such a chamber, many times, by the most learned witches and wizards. It does not exist."*[19]

We do, of course, have a massive advantage over poor Professor Binns—we know from the book title, *Harry Potter and the Chamber of Secrets*, that he is wrong! Nevertheless, his logic is flawed: Simply because the Chamber has not been *found* does not mean that it does not *exist*—especially if, as Seamus Finnigan reminds him, it can only be unsealed by the heir himself. What is more, his grasp of "solid, believable, verifiable *fact*" is flawed: There may be no *proof* "that Slytherin ever built so much as a secret broom cupboard"[20] but there is more than "a shred of evidence"—from the cover-up regarding the Chamber fifty years before to the writing on the wall or the petrification of Mrs. Norris.[21] This evidence is, of course, variously interpretable and far from conclusive but the point is that Binns never even considers the possibility that it might point to the existence of the Chamber. He has come to the evidence with a closed mind, already unswervingly convinced that the Chamber "is a myth! It does not exist."[22] There are, it seems (to borrow from Hamlet), exactly no more and no less things in heaven and earth than are dreamt of in his philosophy.

STAR STRUCK

The metaphysics of Potterworld, therefore, steers firmly away from the brand of Enlightenment ultrarationalism that makes up its mind about things before examining the evidence. But does that mean that Potterworld is an environment in which, to put it bluntly, "anything goes"? Are there no rules? Is nothing impossible? The simple answer is no. As we saw in Chapter Two, examining how she has condensed the qualities of epic into Hogwarts, Rowling herself has a clear idea of what is and is not possible within her creation. "The most important thing, when you're creating a fantasy world, is to set the rules," she told Stephen Fry. "You have no conflict, you have no tension, you have no drama if you have given your characters limitless powers and no barriers. You have to decide, first of all, most importantly, what they *can't* do, way before you decide what they *can* do."[23] As Potterworld is, to all intents and purposes, itself a form of character, Rowling as writer must do what we as readers, or as scientists, must never do: Decide beforehand, a priori, just what is and is not possible.

If Professor Binns represents the intransigence of the hard-line ultrarationalist skeptic, the opposite approach in metaphysical terms is taken by Professor Trelawney, the beads-and-bangles Divination teacher. Even before she is properly introduced as a character in *Azkaban*, her branch of magic—with its drowsy perfumed rooms, tea leaves, palmistry, crystal balls, inner eyes and astrology—has been castigated: Fortune-telling, Hermione explains, is judged by Professor McGonagall to be "a very imprecise branch of magic."[24] After Trelawney has dramatically predicted Harry's death during their first lesson, McGonagall explains, "Sybill Trelawney has predicted the death of one student a year since she arrived at this school. None of them has yet died. Seeing death omens is her favorite way of greeting a new class."[25] If we are tempted to believe, however, that there is something serious beneath such dramatic teaching techniques, we are soon disabused of that notion. By *Goblet of Fire*, after one year of Divination lessons—and, it must be admitted, one real prediction—Harry has "come to the conclusion that her brand of fortune-telling was really no more than lucky guesswork and a spooky manner."[26]

"You know," said Ron, whose hair was on end because of all the times he
had run his fingers through it with frustration, *"I think it's back to the old
Divination standby."*

"What—make it up?"

"Yeah," said Ron, sweeping the jumble of scrawled notes off the
table, dipping his pen into some ink and starting to write.[27]

Though he accidentally predicts his own drowning twice, as Hermione points out, and has to correct the second occurrence to being
trampled by a rampaging Hippogriff, Ron nevertheless gives his as-
signment in to Professor Trelawney, as does Harry, who predicts his
own death by decapitation. They are amused when they receive top
marks and have their inventions read out to the class, "But they were
less amused when she asked them to do the same thing for the month
after next; both of them were running out of ideas for catastrophes."[28]
(Just how Harry can be expected to complete his homework without a
head is a mystery, although Sir Patrick Delaney-Podmore could no
doubt give him some pointers.)

It isn't just her students who doubt the value of Professor
Trelawney's subject, however. There is a massive, ill-disguised rift
between her and Professor McGonagall, perhaps the most fiercely
logical and surely the most Hermione-like member of staff. (The surprise is not that Hermione drops Divination but that she takes so long
to do so; it will be even more surprising if she does not follow
McGonagall in becoming an Animagus before the saga ends.)
Professor McGonagall is scathing about Divination, and Trelawney
in particular.

We could, therefore, be forgiven for thinking that Rowling is not
an avid reader of her weekly newspaper horoscope. However, we
would perhaps be a little too hasty to assume that she simply writes off

astrology altogether. The indications are that, as a literary and heuristic device, she does not. Not only does an unwittingly entranced Professor Trelawney correctly predict the renewed defection of Wormtail in *Azkaban*, but the centaurs—traditionally seen as sky-watching beasts with little interest in the world around them: as Hagrid puts it, "Ruddy star-gazers. Not interested in anythin' closer'n the moon"[29]—read the stars accurately enough to know that something evil is afoot in *Sorcerer's Stone*, and to warn Harry who the real culprit is behind the plot to steal the stone.

As we saw in Chapter One, of course, she is not alone in refusing to reject astrology entirely. Matthew's Gospel, with its geographically misguided astrological wizards eventually arriving at the scene of the nativity, is equally reticent about condemning astrology out of hand. So, revealingly, is Lewis, whose Narnia adventure *Prince Caspian* approvingly features astrology from both stargazing centaurs like Glenstorm and the future-predicting tutor and unofficial "Astronomer Royal," Doctor Cornelius.

> *There was no difficulty in picking out the two stars they had come to see. They hung rather low in the southern sky, almost as bright as two little moons and very close together.*
>
> *"Are they going to have a collision?" he asked in an awestruck voice.*
>
> *"Nay, dear Prince," said the Doctor (and he too spoke in a whisper). "The great lords of the upper sky know the steps of their dance too well for that. Look well upon them. Their meeting is fortunate and means some great good for the sad realm of Narnia. Tarva, the Lord of Victory, salutes Alambil, the Lady of Peace. They are just coming to their nearest."*[30]

Lewis's view of the stars and their role in Narnia is based on the worldview integral to the Medieval and Renaissance literature he studied and taught professionally—a worldview in which the sun, the moon, the planets and the stars orbited the (spherical) earth, and in which, as he explains in *The Discarded Image*, a book based on his Cambridge lectures, "each sphere, or something resident in each sphere, is a conscious and intellectual being, moved by 'intellectual love' of God."[31] This explains the otherwise extraordinary figure of Ramandu in *The Voyage of the Dawn Treader*, who is, as a completely astonished Edmund exclaims, "a *retired* star."[32] It also explains the rationale behind medieval astrology:

> The spheres transmit (to the Earth) what are called Influences—the subject-matter of Astrology. Astrology is not especially medieval. The Middle Ages inherited it from antiquity and bequeathed it to the Renaissance. The statement that the medieval Church frowned upon this discipline is often taken in a sense that makes it untrue. Orthodox theologians could accept the theory that the planets had an effect on events and on psychology, and, much more, on plants and minerals.[33]

What the medieval Church objected to, Lewis explained, was threefold: First, any worship of these stellar Intelligences; second, the lucrative business of astrological predictions (bad news for those present-day astrologers who can command six- and seven-figure salaries from national newspapers); and third, what he calls "astrological determinism"—the idea that the influence of the stars could determine what happens on earth, almost to the point of excluding free will and human moral choices.

On all three points but especially on this last one, Lewis, the Bible and Rowling seem to be in complete agreement. In Chapter One I suggested that magic functioned in all three as a symbol of power, and that its right use was therefore endorsed while its abuse was attacked. In essence, astrological determinism is the reverse. Rather than imag-

ining that we can control the world, we imagine that it controls us—
that we are the impotent pawns of destiny, drawn along by the irresistible hand of fate. As Lewis explains of the Middle Ages, "Men
were far less prone to think they could control the translunary forces
than to think that those forces controlled them. Astrological determinism, not imitative magic, was the real danger."[34]

In Potterworld, the bankruptcy of this determinism is illustrated
not just by Professor Trelawney's incompetence but especially in the
reaction of the centaurs in *Sorcerer's Stone* to the message contained in
the movements of the planets. The resigned and determinist view is
held by Bane, who opposes any action that could "set ourselves
against the heavens." The opposite view is taken by Firenze, who
feels that it is not "the heavens" that they will set themselves against
by helping Harry but "what is lurking in this forest": namely,
Voldemort. The effect of their radically different approaches to astrological phenomena is that while Bane will stand aside and watch as
Voldemort does "monstrous things" (such as killing unicorns) in his
return to power, Firenze will fight "with humans alongside me if I
must."[35] For Bane, it is all over bar the shouting; for Firenze, the eventual outcome is far from certain and there is still everything to play
for. As he tells Harry, "The planets have been read wrongly before
now, even by centaurs. I hope this is one of those times."[36]

None of this implies, of course, that we should engage in the practice of astrology, whatever form it might take. But we need to note
that in Potterworld, as in Narnia (or, indeed, the medieval Church),
the heavens are portrayed as the arena where truth can be discerned as
well as error conveyed. Rowling's handling of astrology may therefore be seen as another example of her inviting us to think twice about
the cultural assumption of the Enlightenment that only science is worthy of respect.

IT'S A KIND OF MAGIC

It is best, then, to see the metaphysics of Potterworld as balanced between the ultrarationalism of Binns and the flakiness of Trelawney. Joanne Rowling sets definite limits on what is possible within her creation, though she draws these limits widely and uses them, I believe, to challenge those who would draw the limits of reality in our *own* world too narrowly. Her creation and outlook is, on the whole, openminded, and will encourage young as well as older readers to keep an open mind and examine extraordinary claims on their evidence, not pontificate a priori on whether they are true or not.

One further aspect of Potterworld's metaphysics perhaps invites investigation. There is a sense in which Rowling has gradually subverted her creation as she has progressed through the series, introducing mundane elements into Potterworld which serve to undermine the very fabric of its magicality. Hogwarts, for example, began the series as an effectively "Unplottable" castle in an undisclosed part of the country—it is now seemingly a "moldering old ruin," at least to the Muggle eye, somewhere in Scotland. In part, the subversion is a result of Rowling's own inventiveness: As the books have gone on, so not only have they got longer but Potterworld itself has become more and more detailed and complex. Things that were once mysterious and mystical have come into sharper focus, and in doing so have been divested of some of their magical properties. But I can't help feeling that some of this is also deliberate, as if Rowling is almost mocking her creation and bringing it down to size.

The most obvious example is the introduction, in *Goblet of Fire*, of the elfin domestic staff. When we first encounter the magnificent Great Hall and the start of year banquet in *Sorcerer's Stone*, the provision of all the different types of food seems as effortless and enchanted as the bewitched ceiling. Lavish and sumptuous dishes appear and disappear not just *as if* by magic but actually *by* magic, conjured from who knows where seemingly by a wave of Dumbledore's wand. By the end of *Goblet of Fire*, of course, we know *exactly* where they have been conjured from—the Hogwarts kitchens, dutifully staffed by elves, situated directly below the Great Hall itself. The dishes are laid out beforehand on five (Rowling only mentions four but there must presumably be another table for the staff) tables in the kitchens, identical to those in the banqueting hall above, and are sent up (by the magical equivalent of a dumbwaiter) at the appropriate moment. The Ministry of Magic forbids elves to have magic wands, though they do seemingly have an innate amount of magic themselves anyway, so the majority of work done on preparing food for the feasts would appear to be manual.

The elves seem to be only too happy in their work (assuming they are not simply historically brainwashed to enjoy their enslavement, as Hermione seems to think), and they *are* indeed magical creatures; but it is surely an act of subversion—of undoing the myth and undermining the magic—to turn a seemingly magical phenomenon into one that is, except for a conjuring trick at the end and the sheer quantity and staggering quality of the food, very much like any other school dinner: hard work for a largely invisible and undervalued team of workers. And, of course, it is not just in the kitchens where the house-elves seem to have been unobtrusively "working like house-elves" ("It's just an expression," said Ron hastily).[37] As Nearly Headless Nick explains, "They come out at night to do a bit of cleaning . . . see to the fires and so on . . . I mean, you're not supposed to see them, are you? That's the mark of a good house-elf, isn't it, that you don't know it's there?"[38] Judging by their complete absence in the first three books, it would seem that Hogwarts' house-elves are very good indeed.

A second example of Rowling's subversive tendency is the de-mystification that surrounds the whole area of magic. This is a tendency that has been there right from the start but has grown and matured as the series has progressed. The idea of a magician's apprentice or a school for witchcraft is far from new, any more than the idea that the magic arts can be learned—the magic of Prospero in Shakespeare's *The Tempest* is predominantly book learning, for example. However, Rowling's creative imagination has imbued it with a sense of reality that has simultaneously made Hogwarts School of Witchcraft and Wizardry a vibrant literary device and given magic an almost unglamorous edge. From the ordinariness of the first-year required text books (most notably Miranda Goshawk's *The Standard Book of Spells (Grade 1)* and Bathilda Bagshot's *A History of Magic*)—as against the far more exciting *Monster Book of Monsters*—to the instruction that 'all pupils' clothes should carry name tags,"[39] Rowling seems to have gone to great lengths to ensure that her fantastic creation is carefully tempered with a rich vein of the positively dull and familiar. The fact that Hogwarts lies squarely in the literary tradition of British boarding school stories (most famously exemplified in *Tom Brown's Schooldays*) further serves to demythologize the magic.

It is as if she wants us to enjoy magic but not too much. In entering Potterworld, we have almost stepped through the looking glass into a world where what we normally think of as magical is actually mundane, and what we think of as mundane is magical. Ron has a pile of comics in his bedroom, for example, featuring not magical superheroes but *The Adventures of Martin Miggs, the Mad Muggle*. His father, meanwhile, although remarking with a note of amused perplexity that Muggles will "go to any lengths to ignore magic, even if it's staring them in the face,"[40] is endlessly fascinated with basic technology:

Mr. Weasley liked Harry to sit next to him at the dinner table so that he could bombard him with questions about life with Muggles, asking him to explain how things like plugs and the postal service worked.

"Fascinating!" he would say, as Harry talked him through using a telephone. "Ingenious, really, how many ways Muggles have found of getting along without magic."[41]

The more complete and detailed Potterworld becomes, the more "exotic" the Muggle world of readers becomes by comparison. The net effect is to make us readers laugh at it, to wonder at it and to view it differently. This is true when those in Potterworld are talking about the Muggle world and when Rowling introduces layers of mundanity into the magical world. There, our day-to-day mundanities seem absurd and amusing—like Rita Skeeter's tabloid journalism; and the more they are exposed in Potterworld the more we find ourselves thinking about our own world in a new light.

In many ways, the mocking of magic and its increasing elaboration go hand in hand. It is as if the more serious things become, the more necessary it is to take some of the air out of the sails. For example, while the ingenious, playful mock Latin of the first books ("*Petrificus Totalus*," the spell for what Hermione calls "the full Body-Bind,"[42] and "*tarantallegra*" which forces Harry's legs to do a quick-step)[43] has given way to a greater amount of real Latin in the later books ("*Expecto patronum*" means "I look for a protector"; "*Crucio*" means "I torture"; "*Accio*" means "I summon"), there is still considerable fun to be had: "*Engorgio*," for instance, sounds far better than the technically correct "*accresco*," and Avada Kedavra is surely meant to carry overtones of the Latin cabalistic charm "abracadabra," now the standard magic word, with perhaps a deathly hint of "cadaver" added for good measure.[44] Rowling's use of Latin as the official language of magic—rather than the rhyming couplets that did for

Shakespeare's "weird sisters" in *Macbeth*, not to mention *Bewitched* and *Sabrina*—gives the incantations of Potterworld a seriousness they might otherwise lack; but I can't help feeling that her decision to use Avada Kedavra, almost the epitome of magical innocuousness, for the most awful spell of all was motivated by a desire for readers not to take the death spell *too* seriously.

There are many other examples of what could be construed as subversion. Broomsticks, for instance, would appear to be innately magical creations but the immediate introduction of the magical equivalent of high-tech Quidditch racing brooms—the Nimbus Two Thousand and the Firebolt—make them at once both alluring and mundane. The wizard world is, it seems, subject to the same built-in obsolescence as the Muggle world when it comes to technological advancement and fashion. Harry's "Broomstick Servicing Kit"—complete with its High-Finish Handle Polish, silver Tail-Twig Clippers and *Handbook of Do-It-Yourself Broomcare*—adds to the impression of magical mundaneness. If an enchanted broomstick still needs manual tailoring, just how much is magic and how much is craftsmanship?

A similar question surrounds the idea of magical practice in general. How much of it is, as Hermione suggests, "Books! And cleverness!"[45] and how much comes down instead to the magical maturity and charisma of the wizard using the spell? The existence of Hogwarts reinforces the idea that magic not only *can* but *must* be learned and right from the start this is tempered with both the innate *presence* of magic (Harry's hair regrowing in a single night) and the innate *absence* of magic (caretaker Filch is a squib—"someone who was born into a wizarding family but hasn't got any magic powers"[46]—and his efforts to learn magic from a Kwikspell course are singularly lacking in any success).

The nature of magic in Potterworld would seem to be that it is accepted as normal only to be subverted. In the end, this leads perhaps to one of the most important conclusions of Potterworld: that Hogwarts is a place of education, and education is not fundamentally about feeding children information but about using information to develop their characters. Consequently, the metaphysics of Potterworld does not so much demand that we believe "six impossible things before breakfast"[47] as invite us to become the kind of people (like Harry, Ron and Hermione) who question the accepted cultural wisdom that science alone can lead us to reality. For Christians wishing to mount a challenge to the closed-mindedness of modernity, Rowling has proved an unexpected—yet welcome—ally.

chapter six

THE BEGINNING

RESPONDING TO POTTERWORLD

As Hagrid had said, what would come, would come . . . and he would have to meet it when it did.[1]

Potterworld is not just a series of children's books: It has become a true cultural icon, and one that has successfully translated into dozens of diverse national and subnational cultures. It connects with something intrinsic to the human spirit, uniting in their admiration and deep enjoyment people from vastly different social and cultural backgrounds. To put it bluntly, literally millions and millions of people, the world over, identify with "the boy who lived."

Like it or not, Christians absolutely *must* take this fact seriously when deciding how to respond to Potterworld. One response would be (as we have seen) to condemn the Potter series as ungodly and dangerous. But a clear and unadorned denunciation, even if it were merited—and I hope it is obvious from what I have written so far that I do *not* believe it is merited—would be guaranteed only to alienate or infuriate those people we might hope to influence. Its effect would be to reinforce the impression, which the Church so often unwittingly gives, that God is implacably opposed to anything his creation might actually enjoy. Damn Harry Potter, in other words, and we instantly appear to be damning alongside him the very people we are trying so hard to reach. Almost without exception, such "shoot first and ask questions later" approaches do far more harm than good. At best, we look foolish and prejudiced; at worst, we drive an unnecessary wedge between Potter fans and the Gospel (which we represent) through the insensitivity of our response.

In simple terms, then, our response to Potterworld—as individual Christians and as the Church—needs to be positive and nuanced. That doesn't mean that we have to be uncritical. It means that our criticism must be the concerned and compassionate criticism of a friend, not the spiteful and self-righteous criticism of a foe.

"WE TOO ARE HIS OFFSPRING"

The apostle Paul famously adopted this approach not simply as a Jew preaching a message to his fellow Jews that included some inherent criticism but equally in the message he preached to predominantly Gentile audiences. Those letters of his which have been passed down to us, for example, (almost a third of the New Testament documents) are essentially the concerned and compassionate criticisms of a friend. However, we see this approach most clearly and most shockingly displayed in his recorded address to the citizens of Athens in Acts 17.

It is fairly common knowledge that Paul, having accepted the invitation of some of the Athenian philosophers to explain his point of view in the renowned debating chamber of Mars Hill, unpacked his message very sensitively. Not only did he omit all mention of Jesus in his speech (referring to nothing more specific than "a man whom he [God] has appointed") but he based it on the kind of religious knowledge and expression he felt his audience would relate to. The essence of his speech was not that humanity is sinful and in need of a redeemer—something that would pass muster with us but would have made little sense to an Athenian crowd—but simply that God didn't need to live in man-made temples and wasn't dependent on human gifts for food but was the source of all human life. "We ought not to think that the deity is like gold, or silver, or stone, an image formed by the art and imagination of mortals," he told them.[2] Most notably, of course, he made use of an altar inscription he had seen in the city, "To an unknown god,"[3] to support his argument (explaining that what was *unknown* to them was *well known* to him), and quoted approvingly from the work of two renowned pagan poets, the legendary Cretan poet Epimenides and Aratus of Cilicia.

What is less well known or understood is precisely how close to the wind Paul sailed. Athens was famous throughout the ancient world not just for the Parthenon, a massive temple dedicated to the goddess Athena, but also for its half-finished but still very impressive temple to Zeus, who was (in some cases quite literally) the father of the Greek pantheon. In *The Iliad* and *The Odyssey*, Homer calls him the "father of gods and men."[4] If the average Athenian citizen heard someone simply talking about "God," as Paul did throughout his talk, they would most naturally assume that he was talking about Father Zeus. Paul, it has to be said, did little to disabuse them of this notion. In fact in many ways he encouraged it. The two snippets from poems that he quoted both relate not to the God of the Bible or some generic deity but very specifically to Zeus. Epimenides (or someone writing in his name) took issue with those who subscribed to the ancient Greek equivalent of the "God is dead" idea, and who had built a symbolic tomb for Zeus. Addressing Father Zeus directly, he wrote:

You are not dead; you live and abide for ever
For in you we live and move and have our being.[5]

The quotation from Aratus, similarly, is from the opening invocation to Zeus in his poem:

In every way we have all to do with Zeus, for we are truly his offspring.[6]

Far from being neutral or ambiguous poems, in other words, Paul's choice of quotations were clearly linked to Zeus. In using them, he risked people thinking that he was simply identifying his Jewish God, the God of the Bible, with the Greek god Zeus, as if there were no difference.

In fact Paul's strategy was far more canny and critical than this. He established a link in people's minds between God and Zeus in order to influence how they perceived him. In the ancient world, gods were generally thought to live in their temples and enjoy the offerings of food that their devotees brought them. This was a very old view, and although most Greeks were fully aware that their gods equally lived on Mount Olympus and in the heavenly realms, they nevertheless could not shake the view that their temples literally *housed* their gods. Even Jews subscribed to this view—though there is no counterpart in Judaism for the idea that food offerings literally nourished God, Jews both in Jerusalem and throughout the Roman world rightly felt that God's "glory" dwelled in a very special way in the Jerusalem Temple. Paul (who would have added to this that it dwelled most fully in the "temple" of Jesus, and of his Church) deliberately exploited the Greek view that Zeus was greater than the temples dedicated to him.

God, he argued—and by this he knew that his hearers would have thought of Zeus—is not so feeble or powerless that he *really* lives in shrines and temples made by human beings and depends on them for food. Nor is he adequately represented by the splendor and symbolism of golden statues or stone cathedrals built in his image or honor. Such "human ignorance," Paul argued, is beneath us: It belongs to the naïveté of a bygone age. God—and once again his audience would have had Zeus in mind—will sweep it away in his righteous judgment "by a man whom he has appointed." The idea of humans being appointed judges by the gods was not new in Greek mythology, so Paul's audience would have had little trouble following, and agreeing with, his speech up to this point. In fact, we are told, it is only when he mentions the resurrection of the dead that he begins to lose his audience. Some, Acts tells us, "scoffed"—only four years later, Paul admitted to the Christians in Corinth (who were having difficulties believing in the resurrection of the dead themselves) that Jesus' death and resurrection generally seemed like "foolishness to gentiles."[7] But for others his risky strategy paid off: They wanted to know more. By being critically positive about Zeus, and pagan poetry written consciously in praise of Zeus, Paul enabled Gentiles with no real understanding of any of the basic tenets of Judaism or Christianity to come to grips with Christian faith and with its God. Through that, we are told, they "became believers."

If Paul could treat literature about Zeus, the "father of gods and men," in this critically positive way, we—surely—can treat literature about Harry Potter, the "boy who lived," in this same critically positive way. The common ground and shared values between Christianity and Potterworld are considerably greater than those between Christianity and the worship of Zeus. If we can use that common ground, encouraging both children and adults alike to recognize and approve the genuine values and virtues of Potterworld—the positive things I have talked about at some length in this book—then there is a real hope and chance that we will, in time, enable them to see the challenge of the Christian faith, helping them to "become believers" themselves.

The writer of Hebrews called the Jerusalem Temple sanctuary "a mere copy of the true one" in heaven.[8] Appropriating this language, we could see the real virtues of Potterworld as "mere copies" of the "true ones" to be found at the heart of the Christian faith, in Jesus himself. Joanne Rowling may perhaps be none too pleased by this analogy—I have no idea whether she would consider herself a Christian or not—but given the massive success and popularity of the Harry Potter books all over the world, and the sheer quality of the "mere copies" (with which literally tens of millions of people readily identify), it would be utter foolishness for us *not* to use the appropriate elements of Potterworld as a potential resource in our ongoing efforts to help people understand the Christian faith. There is, in my view, absolutely nothing wrong—and a good deal right—with using a "mere copy" if it can enhance people's ability to understand the real thing . . . and keep them amused and entertained in the process. Far from amounting to a denial of the Gospel, the Potter series—through its morality, implicit theology and metaphysics—opens a way to encourage children and adults alike to move beyond the literary creation of Potterworld to ask questions about truth and reality in a way that would have been taboo a generation ago. If this is not opening the door to the Gospel, I don't know what is.

NOTES

INTRODUCTION: THE RIDDLE HOUSE

1. HP2 (J. K. Rowling, *Harry Potter and the Chamber of Secrets*. Bloomsbury, London 1998), p. 48.

CHAPTER ONE: THE DARK MARK

1. HP1 (J. K. Rowling, *Harry Potter and the Philosopher's Stone*. Bloomsbury, London 1997), p. 18.

2. See, for example, the article "School puts a hex on Harry," *The Guardian*, March 29, 2000.

3. "American parents call for ban on 'Evil' Harry Potter," *The Daily Telegraph*, October 14, 1999.

4. South Carolina Board of Education, Columbia, minutes for the meeting of November 10, 1999 (sic), online.

5. *Walpurgisnacht* takes its name from its date, April 30, the eve of the unconnected feast of St. Walpurga. It was a pagan festival in Early Medieval Germany, celebrating witchcraft and the powers of darkness. Its equivalent in the English-speaking world is Halloween, October 31, final day of the Church year and eve of All Saints' Day.

6. Barbara W. Tuchman, *A Distant Mirror: The Calamitous Fourteenth Century* (New York 1978. Papermac, London 1995), p. 43.

7. HP3 (J. K. Rowling, *Harry Potter and the Prisoner of Azkaban*. Bloomsbury, London 1999), p. 101.

8. HP3, p. 117.

9. HP3, p. 117.

10. HP3, p. 140.

11. Mark 3:22.

12. Justin Martyr, *Dialogue with Trypho* 69:7. Translated by R. P. C. Hanson (Lutterworth, London 1963), p. 43.

13. The Babylonian Talmud, *c*. A.D. 500. bSanh. 43a.

14. N. T. Wright, *Jesus and the Victory of God* (SPCK, London 1996), p. 440.

15. Matthew 2:1. The same word is used, negatively, of the "magician and false prophet" Bar-Jesus in Acts 13:6.

16. The three non-Narnia novels—*Out of the Silent Planet, Perelandra* and *That Hideous Strength*—all written earlier, were equally controversial, since they were aimed at adults and written in the then-downmarket genre of science fiction.

17. C. S. Lewis, *The Lion, the Witch and the Wardrobe* (Geoffrey Bles, London 1950), Chapter 15.

18. J. R. R. Tolkien, "On fairy-stories," in *Tree and Leaf* (New edition: HarperCollins, London 2001), p. 10.

19. *Macbeth*, Act I, Scene v.

20. *Macbeth*, Act I, Scene iii.

21. HP1, p. 208.

22. *Macbeth*, Act I, Scene iii.

23. "Harry Potter and the triumph of love" *The Times*, October 19, 2000.

CHAPTER TWO: THE MIRROR OF ERISED

1. HP1, p. 15.

2. C. S. Lewis, "On three ways of writing for children," in *Of This and Other Worlds* (Fount, London 1982), p. 43.

3. ibid., p. 55.

4. C. S. Lewis, "*The Hobbit*," in *Of This and Other Worlds*, p. 94.

5. J. R. R. Tolkien, "On fairy-stories," in *Tree and Leaf*, p. 44.

6. HP2, p. 186.

7. HP4 (J. K. Rowling, *Harry Potter and the Goblet of Fire*. Bloomsbury, London 2000), p. 152.

8. HP1, p. 89.

9. HP1, p. 132.

10. HP4, p. 278.

11. HP4, p. 349.

12. Walter Hooper's Introduction in C. S. Lewis, *Of This and Other Worlds*, p. 13.

13. C. S. Lewis, "It all began with a picture . . . ," in *Of This and Other Worlds*, p. 64.

14. Tolkien refers to this metaphor in *Tree and Leaf*, p. 58.

15. HP1, p. 147.

16. J. R. R. Tolkien, "On fairy-stories," in *Tree and Leaf*, p. 56.

17. ibid., p. 59.

18. Leyland Ryken, *The Liberated Imagination* (Harold Shaw Publishers, Wheaton 1989), p. 113.

19. ibid.

20. For a fuller discussion of the role of alternate worlds, see Francis Bridger, *Opening Windows into Heaven: Imagination, Spirituality and the Growth of Faith* (Aquila Press, Sydney 2001), pp. 18–19.

21. Leyland Ryken, *The Liberated Imagination*, p. 113.

22. HP4, pp. 209–10.

23. First editions printed "Crouch" instead of "Fudge" in the line, " 'Dumbledore, come!' said Fudge angrily," even though Crouch was by then already dead; HP4, p. 503.

24. Reported in "Harry Potter author admits blunder," *The Sunday Times*, November 5, 2000, though the initial (subsequently altered) edition of HP1, p. 136, says that the Slytherin Quidditch captain was in fact a sixth-year student when Harry started at Hogwarts.

CHAPTER THREE: THE MAN WITH TWO FACES

1. HP4, p. 555.

2. 1 Corinthians 13:11–12.

3. Beyers Naudé, in Jim Wallis and Joyce Hollyday (ed), *Cloud of Witnesses* (Orbis, Maryknoll NY 1991), p. 157.

4. C. S. Lewis, *Of This and Other Worlds*, pp. 54–55.

5. In fact in *Sorcerer's Stone*, Black gives Hagrid his motorbike to get Harry to safety. Despite Hagrid's later interpretation of this evidence (HP3, p. 154), it indicates his innocence as early as Chapter One of the first book.

6. HP3, p. 257.

7. HP3, p. 260.

8. HP3, p. 259.

9. Romans 7:19.

10. 1 John 1:8.

11. HP2, p. 245.

12. HP1, p. 131.

13. HP1, p. 130.

14. HP1, p. 120.

15. HP3, p. 265.

16. HP4, p. 35.

17. HP4, p. 457.

18. HP4, p. 188.

19. HP4, p. 189.

20. Matthew 7:13–14.

21. HP4, p. 574.

22. HP2, p. 233.

23. HP2, p. 245.

24. HP4, p. 553.

25. Martin Luther King, *Strength to Love* (1963. Fount, Glasgow 1977), p. 76.

26. From an interview in *Time* magazine, quoted in "Children are safe with Harry Potter, author tells critics," *The Daily Telegraph*, October 18, 1999.

27. HP1, p. 60.

28. HP1, p. 61.

29. HP2, p. 114.

30. HP4, pp. 614–15.

31. HP4, p. 331.

32. HP4, p. 456.

33. HP4, p. 458.

34. HP2, p. 246.

35. HP1, p. 14.

36. Martin Luther King, "A Christmas Sermon on Peace," December 24, 1967, preached in strident opposition to the Vietnam War, in James M. Washington (ed), *A Testament of Hope: The Essential Writings and Speeches of Martin Luther King, Jr.* (1986. HarperCollins, San Francisco 1991), p. 255.

37. How Harry *could* have killed Black with a wand is unclear—seemingly only one curse, Avada Kedavra, kills outright and Moody notes that it "needs a powerful bit of magic behind it—you could all get your wands out now and point them at me and say the words, and I doubt I'd get so much as a nose-bleed"; HP4, p. 192.

38. HP3, p. 275.

39. HP4, p. 457.

40. Sirius Black in HP4, p. 458.

41. HP4, p. 589.

42. HP4, p. 614.

43. Martin Luther King, *Where Do We Go From Here: Chaos or Community?* quoted in Coretta Scott King (ed), *The Words of Martin Luther King* (1983. Fount, London 1985), p. 18.

44. HP4, p. 615.

45. McGonagall's assessment, in HP3, p. 154.

CHAPTER FOUR: THE DEATH EATERS

1. HP2, p. 233.

2. Acts 20:35.

3. HP1, p. 149.

4. HP4, p. 344.

5. C. S. Lewis, in Walter Hooper's Introduction to *Of This and Other Worlds*, p. 10.

6. C. S. Lewis, *Of This and Other Worlds*, p. 58.

7. HP3, p. 275.

8. John 15:13.

9. Rowling intimates that Harry himself was the target of Voldemort's murderous designs, lending the event an almost Herod-like slaughter-of-the-innocents import but postpones an explanation of why for a later book; HP1, p. 216. This is the nearest she gets to giving Harry anything remotely resembling a messianic identity. It remains to be seen how, or if, she will develop this as the series draws to its conclusion.

10. HP4, p. 566.

11. HP3, p. 275.

12. Matthew 5:7.

13. Romans 5:8.

14. 1 John 4:9–11.

15. Luke 9:24.

16. HP4, p. 461.

17. Dumbledore explains in HP2, p. 242.

18. HP4, p. 604.

19. HP4, pp. 588–89.

20. HP4, pp. 569–70.

21. Leviticus 17:11.

22. I. Howard Marshall, 1974, quoted in Christopher M. Tuckett, "Atonement in the NT," in David Noel Freedman (ed), *The Anchor Bible Dictionary* (Doubleday, New York 1992), vol. I, p. 518.

23. The English term is literally derived from its constituent parts (at-one-ment), but the Hebrew and Greek terms used in the Bible relate to sacrifice, redemption and salvation in far more diverse and general ways.

24. HP3, p. 140. Hagrid characterizes his release from Azkaban as "like bein' born again"; HP3, p. 164.

25. HP2, p. 221.

26. HP1, p. 99.

27. HP4, p. 605.

28. HP4, p. 579.

29. HP1, p. 215.

30. *Hamlet*, Act III, Scene i.

31. HP4, p. 605.

32. HP4, p. 566.

33. HP2, p. 242.

34. Micah 6:8.

CHAPTER FIVE: THE JOURNEY FROM PLATFORM NINE AND THREE-QUARTERS

1. HP1, p. 68.

2. Karl Marx, "Toward a Critique of Hegel's *Philosophy of Right*: Introduction" (1844), in David McLellan (ed), *Karl Marx: Selected Writings* (Oxford University Press, Oxford 1977), p. 64.

3. J. R. R. Tolkien, "On fairy-stories," in *Tree and Leaf*, p. 60.

4. Quoted in Sallie McFague, *Metaphorical Theology: Models of God in Religious Language* (SCM Press, London 1982), pp. 75–76.

5. HP1, p. 10.

6. HP1, p. 69.

7. HP1, pp. 70–71.

8. St. Anselm, *Proslogion*, 154–55.

9. Alan Lightman, *Dance for Two* (Bloomsbury, London 1996), p. 104. Feynman's comment is recalled on p. 106.

10. HP3, p. 123.

11. HP4, p. 148.

12. HP4, p. 87.

13. HP4, p. 148.

14. Newt Scamander (J. K. Rowling), *Fantastic Beasts & Where to Find Them* (Bloomsbury, London 2001), p. xiv.

15. E.g., Numbers 23:22, Psalm 22:21. Modern translations read "wild ox." Rowling oddly borrows the transliterated Hebrew word *Re'em* to describe an Assyrian

mythical beast, displaced and embellished: "extremely rare giant oxen with golden hides . . . found both in the wilds of North America and the Far East"; *Fantastic Beasts*, p. 36.

16. *Fantastic Beasts*, p. xvii.

17. *Fantastic Beasts*, p. xvii.

18. *Hamlet*, Act I, Scene v.

19. HP2, pp. 114–15.

20. HP2, p. 115.

21. Caretaker Filch's snooping and sneaky cat is, incidentally, named very appropriately after the selfish, spiteful character in Jane Austen's *Mansfield Park*.

22. HP2, p. 115.

23. Interview aboard the Hogwarts Express locomotive during the publicity tour for *Goblet of Fire*, downloaded from the website of publisher Bloomsbury, summer 2000.

24. HP1, p. 190.

25. HP3, p. 84.

26. HP4, p. 177.

27. HP4, p. 195.

28. HP4, p. 206.

29. HP1, p. 185.

30. C. S. Lewis, *Prince Caspian: The Return to Narnia* (Geoffrey Bles, London 1951), Chapter 4.

31. C. S. Lewis, *The Discarded Image: An Introduction to Medieval and Renaissance Literature* (Cambridge University Press, Cambridge 1964), p. 115.

32. C. S. Lewis, *The Voyage of the Dawn Treader* (Geoffrey Bles, London 1952), Chapter 14.

33. C. S. Lewis, *The Discarded Image*, p. 103.

34. C. S. Lewis, *The Discarded Image*, p. 202.

35. HP1, p. 188.

36. HP1, p. 189.

37. HP4, p. 197.

38. HP4, p. 161.

39. HP1, p. 52.

40. HP2, p. 34.

41. HP2, p. 37.

42. HP1, p. 198. Both words do, however, derive from medieval Latin; the classical Latin for "petrify" is *lapidesco*.

43. HP2, p. 144. A *tarantella* is a southern Italian dance, almost manic in its style, thought in medieval times to be either a result of or a cure for the bite of the tarantula spider (itself named after the city of Taranto). Tarantism is the uncontrollable impulse to dance. *Allegro*, of course, is the Italian musical term for quick and lively.

44. Not all of the Latin of the later books is quite right: *Reducio*, for example, should be *reduco*, or better still *deminuo* while *Imperio* should be *impero* and *Imperius* should be *imperium*.

45. HP1, p. 208.

46. HP2, p. 110.

47. The White Queen, in Lewis Carroll, *Through the Looking Glass* (London 1872), Chapter 5.

CHAPTER SIX: THE BEGINNING

1. HP4, p. 636.

2. Acts 17:29.

3. Acts 17:23. Paul may perhaps have taken a minor liberty with the inscription: Two pagan writers from the next century make reference to there being altars to "unknown gods" (plural) in Athens.

4. For example: *The Iliad*, I, 545; *The Odyssey*, I, 30.

5. Quoted in F. F. Bruce, *The Book of Acts*. NICNT (Eerdmans, Grand Rapids 1954. Second Edition, 1988), p. 339. It makes no difference to Paul's argument whether Epimenides actually existed or not, and who wrote the poem. After all, he never cites his source.

6. Quoted in F. F. Bruce, *The Book of Acts*, p. 339.

7. 1 Corinthians 1:23.

8. Hebrews 9:24.

INDEX

The Reverend Dr. Francis Bridger is Principal of Trinity Theological College, Bristol, England, and Visiting Professor of Pastoral Care at Fuller Theological Seminary in Pasadena, California. He is a graduate of Oxford and Bristol universities and has lectured in Australia, England, and the United States. He is the author of a number of books, including *Counselling in Context* and the award-winning *Children Finding Faith*.